The Films of

Jane Fonda

The Films of

Jane Fonda

by George Haddad-Garcia

THE CITADEL PRESS • Secaucus, New Jersey

To my beloved mother, Fresia Garcia Haddad,
and my father, George M. Haddad

Second paperbound printing

Copyright © 1981 by George Haddad-Garcia
All rights reserved.
Published by Citadel Press
A division of Lyle Stuart Inc.
120 Enterprise Ave., Secaucus, N.J. 07094

In Canada: Musson Book Company
A division of General Publishing Co. Limited
Don Mills, Ontario

Manufactured in the United States of America by
Halliday Lithograph, West Hanover, Mass.

Designed by Dennis J. Grastorf

Library of Congress Cataloging in Publication Data

Haddad-Garcia, George.
   The films of Jane Fonda.

   1. Fonda, Jane, 1937–   .   I. Title.
PN2287.F56H3   791.43′028′0924 [B]   81-136
ISBN 0-8065-0754-3   AACR:

ACKNOWLEDGMENTS

   Special thanks to Ronald Milton Boze. Thanks to
Sue Barton at Columbia, Dorothy Denny, Richard
Hudson at Quality First, Sue Kutosh, Richard Scott
at 20th Century-Fox, and Lillian Smith. Thank yous
to the actors and actresses interviewed for this book.
And an inspirational thank you to Jane Fonda:
leading lady and leading woman.

Contents

The Films of

Jane Fonda

Introduction: Jane of Arc

SHE HAS BEEN WIDELY HAILED as our best actress. She is one of the few American performers who is both a superb thespian and a bona-fide superstar. She is the most famous, celebrated Fonda of all—no mean achievement. Not only does she boast the only Academy Award in America's premier acting family, but she has two of the coveted statuettes and has become a perennial Oscar nominee. She has been offered two million dollars for her next film and reportedly signed a three million-dollar contract with ABC—a record for television—for two telemovies. With the possible exceptions of Garbo and Taylor, she is the most publicized actress of all time, and she is the most written-about, talked-about woman in America today. A 1980 poll found her ahead of First Lady Rosalynn Carter in a list of the Most Influential Women in the United States, second only to *Washington Post* and *Newsweek* publisher Katherine Graham.

After a period of unofficial blacklisting by Hollywood, Jane Fonda is now at the pinnacle of her profession and the official top female box-office star in the world. The readership of the cinephile magazine *Take One,* whose average reader views eighty-four films annually, voted her their all-time favorite actor by a considerable margin, ahead of twenty-one past and present greats including Olivier, Katharine Hepburn, Bogart, Brando, Davis, Henry Fonda, and Woody Allen. Middle-American screen watchers share at least some of this enthusiasm, for when NBC telecast *Coming Home*—a film engendered and partly owned by Fonda—in 1979, it garnered one of the largest audiences ever attained by a theatrical motion picture on TV. And *The China Syndrome*—co-produced by Columbia and Fonda's IPC Films—was the biggest hit of 1979 for Columbia.

Fonda is also a producer, a feminist, an activist, a politician's wife . . . a phenomenon. She is a multimillionaire with a distinctly middle-class home and lifestyle, a champion of the masses and especially of the underdog. She is beloved by anti-nuclearists, feminists, pacifists, secretarial organizations, Native Americans (Indians), liberals, movie buffs, and other disparate groups. However, she is also hated and frequently misunderstood by some, even though, according to *People* magazine, she has been "forgiven" by the public.

Phoenix-like, she has risen from the ashes of an aborted career and from the blacklisting caused by her controversial antiwar politicking. Upon her film comeback, her husband, Tom Hayden, explained,

> It's important that Jane be restored to legitimacy now, when she's active, and not in the twenty-first century, which usually happens to controversial people. Lillian Hellman is very "in" now, but she wasn't not too long ago. I'm very impressed by how rapidly Jane's image has started to reverse itself. It's not just her doing: it's a sign that the country has been changing.

Like Ingrid Bergman some two decades before her, Fonda made the costly mistake of betraying an established public image—or rather, images. Audiences were familiar with a cotton-candy star, half-child, in frothy American comedies like *Any Wednesday, Cat Ballou,* and *Barefoot in the Park* and a semi-wholesome sexpot in breathy dramas like *The Chapman Report* and *Walk on the Wild Side* and later in soft-core European romps (some directed by her first husband, Roger Vadim) such as *Joy House, Circle of Love,* and *Barbarella.* None of these images allowed room for firm social or political convictions. "Jack Warner made me dye my hair blond and wear fake eyelashes and falsies," she re-

From a painting by Sue Kutosh.
(Used with the permission of the artist.)

The Fonda features and the Fonda talent would be passed on from Henry to Jane, who by her mid-thirties had equaled and surpassed her father's cinematic achievements. Four of her best-loved Henry Fonda films:
a. Jezebel, *with Bette Davis.*
b. The Big Street, *with Lucille Ball.*
c. My Darling Clementine, *with Cathy Downs.*
d. The Grapes of Wrath, *with Jane Darwell and other cast members.*

called. "He believed that was what a star looked like. Basically, we all came from the same mold."

Surprisingly, Lady Jane (her ironic childhood nickname) was once a tomboy. There was little female influence in her early or later life. In an issue of *Ms.* featuring father-daughter relationships, she stated,

My only major influence was my father. He had power. Everything was done around his presence, even when he wasn't there. It wasn't an unusual way to grow up, but he was also famous, and that increased everyone's sense of his power. . . . I became my father's "son," a tomboy. I was going to be brave, to make him love me, to be tough and strong.

My father was always attracted to strong women, and yet for him women weren't where the action was. I thought women were to be scoffed at and scorned. The highest praise was when a man would tell me, "You're so different from other women." Now, thanks to the Women's Movement and the connections we've all made, I love to work with women and make a special effort to do movies together. . . . I know now that my father respects my work. He's very, very generous in his praise.

Initially, Jane was little more than her father's child, and even as late as the mid-seventies she was sometimes referred to as Henry Fonda's daughter. During the Vietnam war her politics were inevitably compared with his, but rumors of an ongoing feud between them were false, although they did sometimes disagree over the manner of expression of the younger Fonda's ideas. The two have grown closer over the years, and Henry now declares, "I'm in awe of her." They recently realized their dream of doing a movie together. Jane and Peter have already co-starred in the French-made *Spirits of the Dead.*

It is extremely unlikely Jane would ever have become an actress had it not been for her father.

Anthony Perkins and new-to-movies Jane Fonda take time out from a kissing scene in Tall Story.

To some extent, she has patterned her career after his. Like him, she is a genuinely concerned performer:

[Acting] is the only thing I can do, that I'm good at. And I love the fact that I feel like I am and have been many different people. I've always been me, but I have manifested that in different ways. I cannot understand how people, when they become famous, tend to walk through roles. I guess that means they're only in it for the money. I just can't understand it. I always get real nervous whenever I start a film. It's like starting all over again. You really want to do it well.

About her relationship with her father she says:

He's so honest. He's just full of good intentions and integrity. I've even learned to love the things that are strange about him, like how he can say things that are extremely warm and intimate to the press about me, but he won't say them to me directly. . . . A lot is unspoken. He was on TV at the American Film Institute (AFI) Life Achievement Award dinner. The entire country's watching and he's telling a story. It makes me cry even now. He told this lengthy story about how his father didn't want him to become an actor and eventually he did. He did his first play, and his father went to see it. When they came home the sister was kind of critical and the father was sitting there behind his newspaper, and then the father dropped the paper and said, "Shut up. He was perfect."
And then he said something about me, about how people have been critical and how he feels about me. I watched, and I could feel my throat beginning to close up. He's standing up there; I didn't expect him to ever say anything like this. He's talking about me and he says, "And I know if I ever heard anybody say anything about her, I'd say, 'Shut up. She's perfect.'" And he never said anything like that to me. It just wiped me out! . . . I really love him, but it's just that he doesn't tell *me:* he tells the world. Or an interviewer. On the other hand, when I was twenty-three and flexing my own muscles and trying to become independent of him, my anger came through the press rather than dealing with him directly.

Though very much her own woman, Jane Fonda has been heavily influenced and molded by men: first, Henry and, to a lesser extent, Peter; later, Vadim; then an intimate, largely male circle of antiwar activists; and today, Tom Hayden, who helped complete the turnabout of her once-middling career. "I met this guy, this brilliant person I had respected from afar. I'd read Tom's books. It turned out he was very into films, and we'd talk about films in a way I'd never thought about. He had more respect for films than I did." The relationship altered her view of movies and an actor's responsibility. For instance, she determined to play no more hookers. Her role in *Comes a Horseman* was thus reportedly rewritten into that of a self-reliant ranchwoman, the equal of hardy James Caan in the film.

Alan J. Pakula, her director in *Klute, Comes a Horseman,* and *Roll-Over,* declares, "She's so alive, so immediate, so interested, and she has a genuine curiosity about other people and their way of life. She puts herself into each character, and perhaps it stretches her, too."

The superstar is content to live in a very mod-

Jane Fonda made her unspectacular Broadway debut in There Was a Little Girl, *with Sean Garrison.*

est section of Santa Monica, where she does her own shopping and shares cooking and childcare chores with her husband. "I'm famous," she has said. "I earn too much money. These things make me different from the other working women who live on my block, and I don't want to be different from them." Her time is extremely precious and productive, with much scheduling and little or no time for socializing or frivolity. Giving up her own individual time for herself was the most difficult thing she ever had to do, but today she is cheerfully absorbed by her career, family, and activism. "The alienation I felt growing up the way I did is completely gone."

Fonda's life may be viewed as a microcosm of the evolution of the contemporary American woman. Her first three decades were conventional enough—for a celebrity. She then began to question her life, her image, and her self-respect. One fine French morning she asked Vadim, "How can you love and respect me? I'm nothing!"

Her director-husband revealed, "I then discovered something she had been trying to make me understand for a long time. She had the feeling she did not exist as an individual." After the birth of her first child and a solo trip to India, the woman and activist rapidly began to emerge from the girlish star. Her image became increasingly independent of the other Fondas, and her

movies began changing in content and quality. An actress was born.

They Shoot Horses, Don't They? marked her first Oscar-worthy performance, as she grew away from *Barbarella*-like sexuality into feminism. Naturally, her on-set dealings changed too. "In some ways it was easier before, when I was less aware. Things are okay if you remember your place. But if you come to a director, say, with a conceptual suggestion, a principled criticism, you begin to see their eyes glaze over. Better an actress should have a temperamental outburst—that's what's expected."

Her films were no longer simply star vehicles, but weapons geared to modify Hollywood's traditional concept of women. To this end, she had founded her own production company, IPC (Indochina Peace Campaign). IPC's first major effort—six years in the making—was *Coming Home,* in which her Sally Hyde fell in love with a paraplegic vet and evolved subtly but markedly. Fonda didn't, however, participate in the nude

The Fun Couple, *co-starring Ben Piazza, Dyan Cannon, and Bradford Dillman, was Jane Fonda's biggest Broadway flop.*

Posing for an early 1960s advertisement for Lux soap.

lovemaking scene (a double was used). She had become unwilling to bare her body for the camera. But the scene was included at her urging. "It's central to the theme of this movie, which is a redefinition of power and manhood. This man who is paralyzed from the waist down but who can listen and feel and receive pleasure from someone is more of a man in some ways than a man who has his whole body but who is unresponsive to someone else's needs."

Fortunately, Jane's political awareness did not cause her to shun her status as an attractive celebrity, and when the occasion demanded she could be downright beautiful and glamorous, as at the AFI tributes to Bette Davis (which she hosted) and her father, or at various Oscar telecasts (she co-hosted in 1977). At 1979's Academy Award ceremonies she even wore a blond Farrah-style wig.

When she turned forty she was voted one of the best-looking women in the world by European moviegoers. Today she finds no inconsistency in both being liberated and appearing as well-groomed as possible. But by no means is she a clotheshorse, nor is she obsessed by her looks.

By and large, she has practiced frequent moderation and self-restraint in her personal and public lives. A prime example was the 1972 Academy Awards ceremony, the climax of her second nomination, for *Klute.* It had been predicted that she would either renounce the award (as Brando later did) or offer an ill-received political speech (as Vanessa Redgrave later did). Two months previously, she'd sent a Vietnam veteran to accept her Golden Globe, and some had felt that the acceptance speech and the prominent medals on his army tunic had unpleasantly politicized the gala evening. Jane had already proclaimed, "I don't care about the Oscar. I make movies to support the causes I believe in, not for any honors." A few Fonda watchers said she'd not got over losing for *They Shoot Horses, Don't They?* Others felt that she was upset because Redgrave had lost for her spectacular turn in *Isadora,* largely because of her own outspokenness.

Not a few people were hoping and waiting for

Jane Fonda's last play (to date) was Strange Interlude, *which co-starred Geraldine Page and Ben Gazzara and was directed by José Quintero.*

Fonda to win and make a fool of herself. Political motives were inferred from her outfit, a stark black pantsuit, and from her choice of companion, Canadian actor-activist Donald Sutherland. When the winner's name was announced a slight hush fell over the huge auditorium. She rose calmly from her seat and strode to the stage amid a mixture of cheers and boos. She accepted the award and stared at the audience with a momentarily pained expression.

"Thank you. And thank those of you who applauded. . . . There's a lot I could say tonight. But this isn't the time or the place. So I'll just say 'Thank you.'"

Another brief, dumbfounded silence. The orchestra struck up a triumphant tune, and the audience sagged back into their seats, disappointed either that she hadn't embarrassed herself or that she hadn't made the most of a singular opportunity to air her views to a worldwide audience.

"Nature supports a balance," she has explained, "and so do I, because there's too much gray for anyone to see life in only black and white." Friends say moderation is one of her cherished principles, even if she veers from it now and then. At the height of her Vadim period she did far fewer nude scences than many people believe, and at her most housewife-spar-

15

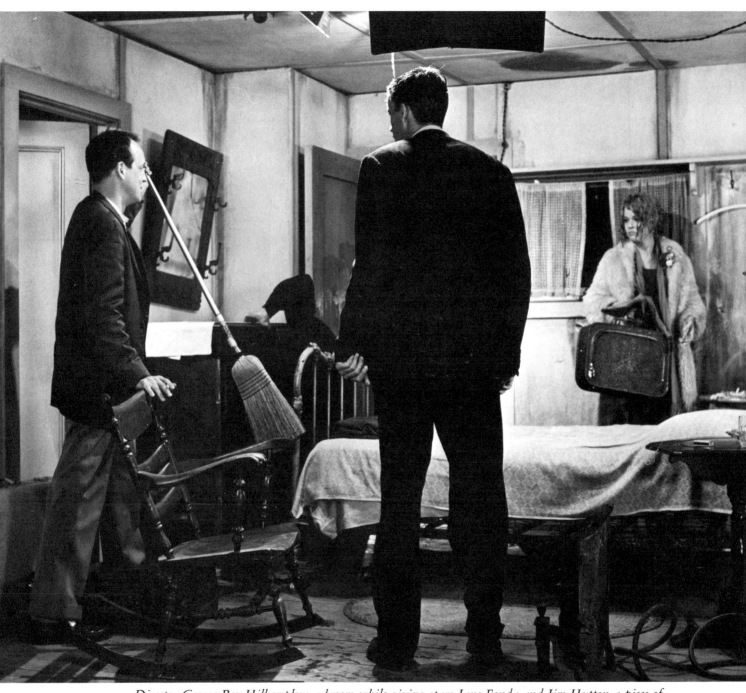

Director George Roy Hill employs a broom while giving stars Jane Fonda and Jim Hutton a piece of technical advice during the filming of Period of Adjustment, *Tennessee Williams's first and last comedy.*

Leading man Jim Hutton chats on the set of Period of Adjustment *with his "bride," Jane Fonda.*

tan in Santa Monica she still leads a balanced, contented life. Maturity has mellowed Jane Fonda but hasn't watered her down. She is the first to say this, pointing to her stepped-up political activities and the firmness of her convictions. Even so, she has moderated her words and appearance and settled gracefully into chosen life roles that include wife and mother.

She has revealed,

I felt lonely a lot for the first thirty years of my life. The scars will never go away, but I began to look for solutions. I began to work in a political way. I may have lost a reputation and a lot of friends, but essentially what I lost was cynicism. I moved from my sex-kitten image to a very different place. . . . I found hope. And I am not lonely now. I am a very happy person, and that's something I never thought I'd be able to say about myself.

Jane Fonda: Star and Actress

JANE SEYMOUR FONDA was known for many years as Henry Fonda's daughter. She was his first child. Peter came a few years later. Then, much later, when Henry wed wife number three—out of a total of five—he adopted a baby daughter named Amy.

Jane's mother was Frances Seymour Brokaw, the youthful widow of George Brokaw, a multimillionaire who had been married to Clare Boothe (pre-Luce). Of distinguished lineage, Frances was the oldest of seven children, born in

Massachusetts in 1905. She took business courses at Katharine Gibbs in Boston, then met Brokaw, who was neither a self-made man nor a consistently sober one. They married in 1931, and in 1935, the year Henry Fonda made his first film (*The Farmer Takes a Wife,* with Janet Gaynor), Brokaw died in a Connecticut sanatorium, leaving his widow nearly five million dollars.

Henry Fonda, who had previously been married to actress Margaret Sullavan, married

Jane Fonda shares an observation with co-star Peter Finch and with Robert Stevens, who directed them in an ill-fated venture, In the Cool of the Day.

Frances in 1936, and their first child, Jane Seymour, was born December 21, 1937, in New York City. At one month, the infant and her parents moved to a mansion in Brentwood, Los Angeles. Following World War II, the family moved to Greenwich, Connecticut, and Henry starred in *Mr. Roberts* on Broadway. The marriage had already been deteriorating when Fonda fell in love with twenty-one-year-old Susan Blanchard (the stepdaughter of Oscar Hammerstein II).

Frances suffered a series of nervous breakdowns and was confined to a sanatorium where, on April 14, 1950, she cut her throat and died in her bathroom. Jane was twelve years old at the time and reportedly didn't learn how her mother died until a classmate handed her a magazine ac-

count of the suicide. Peter didn't find out until, at fifteen, he read about it in a Rome barbershop; he had believed their mother had died of cancer.

The name *Fonda* is Italian, but the American Fondas have predominantly Dutch ancestors, for the Fondas of northern Italy long ago emigrated to the Netherlands. The Marchese de Fonda, head of the family in the 1300s in Italy, was a political activist like his female descendant six-hundred-odd years later, who agitated for a republic independent of the church. His politics caused him and his family to leave an Apennine valley for Holland. In 1642, one of the Dutch Fondas emigrated to what became Albany, New

York, and offshoots of the family founded the town of Fonda, New York.

The young Henry Jaynes Fonda, born in Grand Island, Nebraska, in 1905, originally intended to become a writer but got sidetracked into a local Omaha theater, which Marlon Brando's mother had helped organize. He later studied theater in New York City (Bette Davis was a classmate) before moving on to motion pictures and Broadway.

Jane also considered various careers before acting, but one thing was certain: She wanted to do something special with her life and excel at something in which she could express her own burgeoning personality. "I grew up in the shadow of a national monument," she recalled. "I was sweet, polite, the girl next door—everything I felt I wasn't."

She was sent to the best schools (eventually attending Vassar) and surrounded by a governess and servants. She dwelt amid luxury and comfort; yet she has characterized her childhood as somewhat empty. Her father—and each of his wives—was often away, and when he was present, he was not given to displays of affection or excuses for spoiling his children. A widely circulated but unconfirmed story illustrating the tone of Jane's youth reported that her father once abruptly slapped her face after she repeated a word she had overheard on the playground. The word was *nigger.*

The only daughter grew up a tomboy from an early age, equating importance and attention with maleness. She was athletic and competitive with her younger brother, always vying for Henry's time and love. By five, she was a fledgling horsewoman, and she would act out western stories with her brother, usually insisting on playing roles similar to those her father had done in the movies.

Money bought a whole world of childish distractions, but though the Fonda homes were peopled and visited by the famous and near famous, life wasn't always warm there. For a while after their mother's death, Jane and Peter lived with their maternal grandmother, and from thirteen to seventeen Jane attended Emma Willard School in Troy, New York, where she made her

acting debut, in a male role in *Boy with a Cart*. She did other school plays but gave no thought to acting professionally, even after she "blossomed."

Meanwhile, the star of the family went from one triumph to another, and as a teen, Jane got to co-star with him in the Omaha Community Theatre production of *The Country Girl*. They also did *The Male Animal* in summer stock. But still, the young beauty wasn't turned on to acting. At Vassar, she was said to be devoted to pursuing boyfriends and occasionally rebelled against the strict school rules, but she was a top-notch student, learning quickly and with relatively little effort. At last she decided to devote herself to art; after two years of college she went to Paris to study painting and improve her elementary French:

"I moved in with Countess somebody or other. It was a dark, elegant apartment where young ladies weren't supposed to talk at the table. And while I attended classes at l'École de la Chauvierre and worked briefly for George Plimpton on the *Paris Review,* I really played hooky most of the time. When my father found out, I came home."

She worked as a secretary for a while but she was fired when she refused to respond to her boss's advances. Her typing, she has joked, is still rudimentary, but in later years she took up the cause of working women, and she incorporated the secretarial experience into her film *Nine to Five.* In 1958, while attending the Art Students League in New York, she happened on Lee Strasberg's famous Actors Studio. "I went to the Actors Studio, and Lee Strasberg told me I had talent. *Real* talent. It was the first time that anyone, except my father—who *had* to say so—told me I was good. At *anything.* It was a turning point in my life. I went to bed thinking about

23

Henry and Peter Fonda visit glamourpuss Jane on the location shooting of Sunday in New York.

Between scenes of Sunday in New York *Jane Fonda and Robert Culp confer with a visitor to the leading lady's trailer-dressing room.*

acting. I woke up thinking about acting. It was like the roof had come off my life!"

She earned tuition for the Actors Studio by modeling, and before long she was a *Vogue* cover girl. The young woman became the center of attention as speculation mounted whether she would become the second famous Fonda of the movies. But first, she appeared in *The Moon Is Blue,* then hit Broadway's big time in *There Was a Little Girl,* and won the 1960 New York Drama Critics Circle Award and *Theatre World's* award, both as the most promising actress of the season.

Luckily, Jane was temperamentally ill-suited to modeling. She took up acting "because there was a vacuum and I had to work." But she later admitted, "When I first started acting I was genuinely afraid of not being very good. It's one thing to be mediocre if you're Jane Doe. It's quite another if you're Henry Fonda's daughter

and have a lot to live up to." Not until 1979 could she say, "I *like* being an actress—I'm beginning to relish it. In fact, it doesn't threaten me any more. I enjoy it."

There Was a Little Girl was directed by Joshua Logan, an old friend of the Fondas. Although the play received poor reviews and didn't do very well, the aspiring actress became a celebrity overnight. She gave her first major interview to *Life,* which wrote, "Any suspicion that Jane is riding to fame on her father's shoulders is unfounded. Fonda never gave Jane any help or even encouragement. . . . 'Jane has made more progress in one year,' says her surprised and immensely pleased father, 'than I have in 30.' "

The reknowned Brooks Atkinson wrote of her Broadway debut, "Although Miss Fonda looks a great deal like her father, her acting style is her own. As the wretched heroine of an unsavory melodrama, she gives an alert, many-sided performance that is professionally mature and suggests that she has found a career that suits her." Another critic prophesied, "With the budding talent that she displayed, she might become the Sarah Bernhardt of 1990. But she'd better find herself a more genuine play than this one." Another critic summed up the general feeling that "Jane Fonda has a fine future but not in this play."

Jane Fonda poses with Rod Taylor and friends at a Manhattan locale for Sunday in New York.

26

The Films of Jane Fonda

IT WAS HER ACTING COACH, Lee Strasberg, who convinced Jane to tackle Broadway, but after her personal triumph in *There Was a Little Girl,* she didn't need another push. In late 1960 she appeared in *Invitation to a March,* with a sterling cast that included Celeste Holm, Eileen Heck-art, James MacArthur, and Madeline Sherwood. The notices for the play itself were better this time, and Henry's daughter won the critics over again. George Oppenheimer of *Newsday* said that she had "a glow that almost dims the moonlight. Here is surely the loveliest and most gifted

Roger Vadim, who directed Jane Fonda in Circle of Love, *speaks with his principal star and wife-to-be.*

of all our new young actresses," and the *Telegraph's* Whitney Bolton labeled her "by 87 statute miles the handsomest, smoothest and most delectable ingenue on Broadway."

Although she was critic-worthy and viable in box-office terms, it was Jane's looks more than her underexploited talent that attracted attention; the fact that she was a Fonda didn't hurt, either.

By the time she did her third major play, *The Fun Couple,* in 1962, she'd broken into movies via *Tall Story.* But once again, she was a lovely ingenue, and her movie debut was less than dazzling. So was *The Fun Couple,* which lasted all of three performances. The four-character cast included future stars Dyan Cannon and Bradford Dillman, plus Ben Piazza. The *New York Post* provided the obituary: "The most incredible thing about the play is that two such talented young performers as Jane Fonda and Bradford Dillman were willing to appear in the title roles. Even the sight of Miss Fonda in a bikini doesn't rescue *The Fun Couple* from being an epic bore."

In 1963, she did her last play (up to this writing), Eugene O'Neill's *Strange Interlude,* an all-star Actors Studio revival. Star pupil Geraldine Page played the mother of the young man with whom Jane, as Madeline Arnold, fell in love. The *Times* dubbed it a "brilliant revival" and opined that "Jane Fonda happily contributes her vivacity and beauty to the final two acts." Franchot Tone, Ben Gazzara, and Richard Thomas were among the cast, but *Strange Interlude* failed to make much of an impression, even if the star's beauty did impress.

Her director in the play, José Quintero, stated a few years later,

Otto Preminger and Michael Caine share a lighter moment with Jane Fonda on the tense southern set of Hurry Sundown.

producer-director Otto Preminger mulls over a scene from the all-star racial drama Hurry Sundown *with Jane Fonda.*

31

The first time I met Jane she came to read for me at the old Circle in the Square for the part of Emily in *Our Town*. I had her come back twice, as I was impressed, first by her looks, which as everybody knows are quite staggering, but then I was deeply moved by her vulnerability. I did not cast her in the role; she was too individual—Emily had to be everybody. The events were the important thing in *Our Town*. With Jane we see life as it happens to her. We see it through her perspective. I think she is unafraid to see it all, and that's why I keep thinking: What's next?

Despite an auspicious beginning in *There Was a Little Girl,* her next three plays didn't inspire Jane to continue on the stage. Despairing of ever having a hit and challenging material, she gave up the theater, having also turned her back on television, in which she'd made one or two minor appearances.

However, by the time she quit the stage the female Fonda was a bona-fide international movie star. She had become more self-confident but was still frustrated by the art of acting. She stated at the time, "Just to get up in the Actors Studio and do a scene is so hard, mainly because I know that there are people there who have far more talent than I do. I know that I do have something else: I have star quality; I have a personality. I have presence on the stage, which may make me more important than they are. What I have is obvious—it's like a commodity, and it's in demand. But in terms of acting ability, they have more. That's why it's so hard."

She got into the habit of viewing her own

Roger Vadim explains the futuristic set of Barbarella *to star and wife Jane Fonda, in Paris.*

Jane Fonda offers a bit of cake to her husband and director Roger Vadim, after wrapping up the sexy, spacey film Barbarella.

Director Sydney Pollack halts filming of They Shoot Horses, Don't They? *to explain a point to the cast and crew, including Jane Fonda and Michael Sarrazin.*

films several times to judge and criticize her performances. (By contrast, Henry has never liked seeing himself on screen.) Eventually she drifted away from the Actors Studio, but Strasberg's assistant Andreas Voutsinas became her confidant and career advisor, to the displeasure of her father, who was one of several people who distrusted the sensual Greek. Voutsinas was in part responsible for Jane's turning to sexier roles, supposedly so she could distinguish herself and expand her range.

She was still considered the girl next door, a blonde glamourpuss who was America's most famous daughter, a wholesome, harmless star next to the likes of Marilyn or Brigitte. Her movie debut, in 1960, had been in *Tall Story.* (She'd signed a contract with Joshua Logan that later led to mutually cool feelings.) *Tall Story* was a lackluster vehicle, but she turned it into a personal triumph. For years, she had to rise above her material—fluff, comedy, melodrama, and "naughty" French films. Her sixties apprenticeship in mostly mediocre films had advantages and disadvantages. On the one hand, she wasn't an instant superstar with tailor-made vehicles like, for example, Streisand or Audrey Hepburn. Because her image and successes weren't so clearly defined, Fonda was able to grow artistically and not be hindered by the stereotyping from which other superstars suffered.

In box-office terms, several female stars were ahead of Fonda in the early sixties. She was not a top draw until the late sixties, with pictures like *Cat Ballou, Barefoot in the Park,* and *Barbarella.* But little by little, she surpassed other actresses of her generation artistically, until by the late seventies she was widely acknowledged as the best in the land.

A drastic change in her professional and personal life occurred when she met Roger Vadim and acted in his *Circle of Love,* then fell in love with him and married him. The all-American girl moved to France, where she acquired an earthier image and did seminude scenes in her husband's films while supposedly living in decadent splendor.

Vadim, whose original name was Roger Vladimir Plemiannikov, was of Russian-French par-

Jane Fonda gracefully accepts her first Academy Award, for Klute, *at the forty-fourth awards show in Hollywood.*

entage and had risen to fame (or notoriety) in the mid-fifties as the man who discovered and molded Brigitte Bardot, previously a pouty brunette starlet. They married and had no offspring; then they divorced but continued working together. Vadim went on to shape the careers of beauties like Annette Stroyberg and Catherine Deneuve.

By American standards Vadim's morals were reprehensible, for he didn't always marry his live-in loves; he had a child by Catherine De-

37

neuve but never wedded her. He did marry Jane Fonda, whom he called Kiki. They later had a daughter whom they named Vanessa.

Vadim found that

living with Jane was difficult in the beginning. . . . She had so many—how do you say?—bachelor habits. Too much organization. Time is her enemy. She cannot relax. Always there is something to do—the work, the appointment, the telephone call. She cannot say, "Oh, well, I'll do it tomorrow." This is her weakness.

Her strength? Jane has a fantastic capacity for surviving. She learned long ago how to be lonely. She can be very—in French we say *solide*. For me, what was attractive was her attention to other people. She knows how to listen. This is so rare, especially for a woman. She opens her mind; she tries to understand.

Fonda's publicity mushroomed after she met Vadim, and the public often assumed the worst, labeling the director a Svengali or a user. Henry Fonda was mistrustful of his new son-in-law, and the press played up the more sensational aspects of the couple's relationship. But insiders revealed that Jane and Vadim, except for their wealth and the circles they moved in, were fairly typical newlyweds, quiet and domestically inclined, with a penchant for privacy. The actress today remains a friend of Vadim, about whom she declines to say anything harsh or critical, having already spoken her piece about his cinematic exploitation of women. After marrying Vadim, she did more European films but frequently returned to the States to do either well-intentioned flops like *Hurry Sundown* (with Faye Dunaway and Michael Caine) and *The Chase* (with Brando and Redford) or popular comedies like those mentioned earlier.

In 1968, Jane became a mother for the first time. Originally, she and Vadim hadn't wanted children. For a long time, she'd felt she didn't get along particularly well with kids, but she later gave the situation serious consideration:

I was thirty, and I thought, "Well, if I'm ever going to do it, I'd better try now or before I know it, I'll be forty, and it will be a lot harder."

In her famous shag haircut and new, casual fashion style, Jane Fonda prepares to play six different roles in a satiric protest titled "Fascinating Woman," for the PBS-TV series Dream Machine.

42

When she learned about her pregnancy:

> I didn't want anyone to know it. I felt so vulnerable. I realized how I had always, strangely enough, rejected femininity because it represented to me vulnerability and a lot of things that scared me. During the process of becoming a mother, I completely overcame this. . . . I just came to terms with myself and my body and my fellow women. Truly, my relationships with women have changed since then and, consequently, with everyone.

The star's need to be competitive with other women in terms of beauty, possessions, and men gradually faded. She became more natural and curious about other people and their problems. Before she gave birth, Jane had a nightmare that her daughter would be born as a ten-year-old replica of Brigitte Bardot. Bardot had predicted that the offspring would be a female born on September 28, 1968. When Fonda gave birth to Vanessa on September 28, Bardot sent a telegram: WHAT A NICE GESTURE OF FRIENDSHIP. French newspapers headlined: VV BORN ON BB'S BIRTHDAY. But although Brigitte and Jane were good friends, Vanessa was supposedly named after another actress, an Englishwoman who was an activist long before Jane.

"Something happened to me while she was growing inside my stomach," explained the new parent. "For the first time in my life, I felt confident as a human being and as a woman, and I'm sure it was because I was finally a mother. I began to feel a unity with people. I began to love people, to understand that we do not give life to a human being only to have it killed by a B-52 bomber or to have it jailed by fascists or to have it destroyed by social injustice. When she was born—my baby—it was as if the sun had opened up for me. I felt whole. I became free."

Shortly after Vanessa's birth, Jane's most famous film to that time was released worldwide. *Barbarella* made millions and further emphasized her sex-symbol image, which she would shortly repudiate. Although sexy and beautiful in *Barbarella,* Fonda was still not a genuine actress. Past thirty, she still hadn't delivered a truly outstanding performance. She had yet to win her peers' respect, which she did in her next full-length film, *They Shoot Horses, Don't They?* It was the first project in which her appearance took a back seat to her hitherto untapped talent.

Besides nursing Vanessa, Jane was working harder than she ever had, turning in her first Oscar-nominated performance. But after it was all over she was still restless. Newer changes were taking place inside her: All the new thoughts, emotions, and experiences she'd been through hadn't yet jelled into a new Jane Fonda.

The turning point came in October 1969, when she left behind the world she knew and headed for India, as several stars had recently done, to immerse herself in a new cosmic experience. She chose India because she knew absolutely nothing about it. She would be cut off and isolated there, fending for herself materially and psychologically. Her childhood friend Mia Farrow had returned from the subcontinent with a new peacefulness. Inspired by her example, Jane departed shortly after Vanessa's first birthday.

Although she had anticipated cultural shock, she wasn't prepared for the overwhelming contrast between India on one hand and Paris and Beverly Hills on the other. "I had never seen people die from starvation or a boy begging with the corpse of his little brother in his arms. . . . I met a lot of American kids there, hippies from wealthy or middle-class families in search of their individualistic metaphysical trips. They accepted that poverty. They even tried to explain it away to me."

Unlike her fellow westerners, she was unable to accept the suffering and gross injustices. She pointed out that it was the social system, a whole way of thinking, that was keeping a majority of people down.

Then Jane visited Sikkim, high in the Himalayas, where her sense of injustice was heightened by a sojourn with the king and queen of Sikkim. The latter was the former Hope Cooke, an American contemporary of Fonda's. The opulence of the royal palace and the rulers' lifestyle contrasted appallingly with the lot of the average citizens, few of whom could feed their families. This and other episodes made the actress acutely aware of the privilege she had been

46

50

reared in, and for the first time her thoughts shifted to—and remained fixed on—ordinary people.

She wished to remain longer but was committed to returning to do publicity for *They Shoot Horses*. She flew from Bombay to L.A., checking in to the posh Beverly Wilshire Hotel and discovering that

> when I woke up in the morning I still had in my eyes the crowds of Bombay, in my nose the smell of Bombay, in my ears the noise of Bombay. My first day back, and I saw those houses of Beverly Hills, those immaculate gardens, those neat, silent streets where the rich drive their big cars and send their children to the psychoanalyst and employ exploited Mexican gardeners and black servants. I'd grown up here, but I'd never looked at it in these terms before. . . . Beverly Hills was as silent and empty and antiseptic as a church, and I kept wondering, *"Where is everybody?"*

Her own country was in a relative state of turmoil, what with a massive antiwar moratorium and the November takeover of Alcatraz Island by a band of Native Americans. Jane found herself following the Native American saga with interest, drawing parallels between their plight and that of the Asian Indians who had fought against the British for control of their own land. After reading an article in *Ramparts* magazine that fanned her fires (her friend Marlon Brando influenced her too), she began speaking out on the issue.

Meanwhile, back at the Beverly Wilshire, Vadim was becoming disenchanted with his wife's moody introspectiveness in the wake of her journey, and her growing involvement with Alcatraz. In addition, after Jane expressed interest in the Black Panthers the relationship between her and her father became more strained, and he suspected she was being manipulated. The fledgling activist's attentions were refocused on her career when she won the New York Film Critics Circle Award as Best Actress for *They Shoot Horses*. She accepted the award appreciatively. "It's the biggest accolade I've ever been

Sporting her "Farrah Fawcett wig" and more conventional evening attire, Jane Fonda gives an emotional acceptance speech (part of it in American Sign Language) upon her second Oscar win, for Coming Home.

51

given. One tries to be blasé about things, but now that it's happened, it's very nice."

Fonda was escorted to Alcatraz Island by Peter Collier, author of the *Ramparts* article. She followed Brando's lead and also allied herself with the controversial Black Panthers. She soon began soliciting monetary contributions for her causes by phone, earning herself the nickname the Mad Caller. While at a party thrown by Liz and Dick she drummed up the nerve and the charm to wheedle a generous check from conservative Taylor.

Jane told everyone who would listen, "I had to find out about what was happening with our own Indians, and I was also curious about the Black Panthers." Her usefulness to those groups

Her hair dyed "Brenda Starr red" for her role in The China Syndrome, *Jane Fonda arrives at one of numerous awards shows in her honor. Hollywood and the moviegoing public had taken her to heart again, more than ever before.*

was limited, however, and she soon added a third to her list: GIs.

She wondered how she could benefit the antiwar movement; then she met Fred Gardner, an antiwar activist hired by Michelangelo Antonioni to write *Zabriskie Point,* his first American movie. Gardner overheard Fonda declare to friends that she wanted to take a cross-country tour to obtain a better feel for her countrypeople. Confounded by the sex symbol's genuine interest in social welfare, Gardner suggested, "Why don't you go to some of the GI coffeehouses?" She admitted she didn't even know what a GI coffeehouse was.

After meeting with several servicemen she decided to pledge herself to the GI cause and the U.S. Servicemen's Fund. She combined her Native American loyalties with her new commitment by marching with 150 Native Americans on Fort Lawton, which had been declared Indian territory. One hundred Native Americans were arrested, and the actress was roughed up and headlined a "troublemaker." The sight of police officers clubbing nonviolent Native Americans incensed her and she announced a tour of Native American reservations and army bases on behalf of a Native American and GI Bill of Rights.

She was received less than royally at most bases she visited. At Fort Lewis she remarked, "Bob Hope was greeted differently by the local branch of the military-industrial complex. But then, I did not come up here to glamorize war or urge young men to fight."

At this point, Fonda invited a friend from France, Elisabeth Vailland, to come to the States and join her odyssey. "It was my first trip to America," said the Frenchwoman, "but on the ride in from the airport I noticed nothing, so intent was I on the voice of my young friend as she spoke of her commitment, her preoccupation with the political conscience that was being born."

Jane took Elisabeth to Hollywood to meet her father and persuade him to take an activist role. She and Vailland spoke of the atrocities that had been described to them by American GIs returning from Vietnam. "I told my father all the

54

things I'd learned. He exploded, 'You don't know what you're talking about. We don't do that. We're American. And even if the soldiers did it they wouldn't talk about it.' So I explained that when they start talking you can't stop them, and he said, 'If you can prove that it's true, I will lead a march to Nixon and confront him.' "

So she invited a former Green Beret sergeant and another vet to her father's Bel Air home. Henry listened, obviously moved by the first-hand comments, then stated sadly, "I don't see what I can do besides what I'm already doing—that is, campaigning for the peace candidates." His lack of direct action may have frustrated Jane, but the pair grew closer as a result of the confrontation. There would be future occasions, though, when her father's patience was tried.

Amid touring Native American reservations Jane had to fly back for the Academy Award ceremony. She'd been highly acclaimed for her portrayal in *They Shoot Horses,* but Hollywood felt she'd spoiled her chances for the Oscar by becoming so vocal and controversial. One friend opined, "A pure case of political prejudice. The whole country knew that she should have had [the Oscar]. It was no contest. They kept it from her because they were afraid she'd get up and make a political speech." The film establishment was not yet used to politicized stars, and Fonda made no comment about having lost.

1970 proved a watershed year for her. After touring the country and speaking her piece on just about everything, she was ready to get back to making movies, specifically *Klute* for Alan J. Pakula and Warners. But although she would play her first call girl she told the world she was no longer a member of the sex-symbol market:

It's very hard to find a man like Vadim. He helped me a lot. . . . I don't know why people always saw me as a sex symbol even before Vadim. Then Vadim came and emphasized the whole thing. I say it without rancor, for it was not Vadim who imposed that on me. I allowed it to happen. Vadim does not realize he's exploiting sex, that he's perpetuating the idea of women as sex objects. I was so used to being considered a sex symbol that I began to like it. I didn't expect people to treat me as a person who

thinks, but when I went to the Indians and I came in contact with the Panthers, the GIs, my new friends, I realized they were treating me as a person. This was so beautiful that I began to feel uncomfortable with people who still considered me a doll. It completed my own personal revolution, and Vadim was the first victim of it.

Soon after came the decision to split with "the crazy Russian," as she now affectionately called him. The Frenchman admitted in his *Memoirs of the Devil* that Fonda was the only woman he ever truly loved. He also revealed it had been "very difficult being married to a Joan of Arc." Nevertheless, the divorce was amicable, and much to his relief, he could see Vanessa as often as he wished. Since she would be traveling extensively, Jane temporarily left their daughter in his charge.

Though *Klute* was no more significant than the average thriller, its star managed to infuse it with social comment. Prostitutes, she felt, "are the inevitable product of a society that places ultimate importance on money, possessions, and

Robert Redford and Jane Fonda react to a humorous remark by director Sydney Pollack, on the Nevada location of The Electric Horseman.

Jon Voight, her Coming Home *co-star and friend, presents Jane Fonda with the World's Favorite Actress award at the Golden Globes awards ceremonies in 1980.*

competition." She did research by hanging out and rapping with East Side call girls like the one in the script. Her exposure to prostitution may have aided her performance, but it also made her more aware of sexism. She questioned why, other than her political affiliate Elisabeth Vailland, she had never had a close female friend. She said of the system,

> It doesn't respect human life. It makes you a slave, and it's wrong. Look at what it does to women. Just look at the TV ads. It pits women against each other. It's like a disease. Ninety-five percent of the women in this country are brainwashed by this. They truly believe they only exist as a function of how they look, how they dress, of the kind of men they're with.

Her role as Bree Daniel completed, she returned to the lecture-inspection circuit. Upon her return to the States from Fanshaw College in Canada, her suitcase full of organic vitamin pills became a center of controversy. She used the pills to supply herself with much-needed nutrition, since she seldom ate regular meals. But when Customs Inspector Troiano of Cleveland saw them he informed her she would be detained until his supervisor arrived from downtown. To no avail, she explained what the pills were.

Special Agent Edward Matuszak arrived while Jane was phoning a friend in Boston to inform him of her plight. Matuszak allegedly ordered her to hang up. She complied. She was held in the customs office until Matuszak's superior could be found. After several hours of not being allowed to leave the room, she became extremely uncomfortable, owing to a full bladder. She requested use of the restroom, but Matuszak wouldn't comply until two matrons arrived to search her. He believed she would "destroy possible evidence of contraband drugs she might possess on her person." The agent finally left the customs office but told a policeman to keep an eye on her while he made a call from the immigration office next door. Jane slipped out and scurried to the bathroom. Matuszak intercepted her and ordered her back. On the verge of tears she shouted, "What do you want me to do, pee all over the floor?"

A loud quarrel ensued, and according to Matuszak, the actress tried to punch him. She was arrested for "striking a federal officer," but when she indignantly replied that she hadn't hit him, Matuszak turned to Troiano and the policeman and asked, "Did you see it?" The two men nodded agreement with their superior.

Two more policemen joined the scene, eager to view a star in the flesh. In desperation she headed for the restroom again. Rebuffed, she flailed out at her tormentors, garnering an additional charge of assaulting Peiper, the first policeman. A subsequent search disclosed that all she had had on her—in her handbag—was sleeping pills and tranquilizers. Unfortunately, the incident was widely misrepresented and resulted in headlines like JANE FONDA ARRESTED: ACCUSED OF SMUGGLING DRUGS, KICKING OFFICER.

This was but one of various planned incidents to blacken her name; J. Edgar Hoover and the FBI eventually joined in, trying to pin on her a phony assassination threat against Nixon, to be "reported" in *Variety* and then "leaked" to the national press.

The Cleveland episode haunted Jane for a long time; yet she vowed to intensify her social and political activism. One of her friends, Doctor Howard Levy, a former army captain jailed for declining to train Vietnam-bound soldiers, suggested a new project for her. "I suggested something like a Bob Hope–type show, touring the bases and giving the troops some really first-class entertainment—sort of an alternative Bob Hope show."

The idea caught her fancy, and she enlisted the talents of several friends, including lover and co-star Donald Sutherland. The F.T.A. (euphemistically subtitled Free the Army) show was eventually captured on film, one of her least successful ventures. Several of her F.T.A. colleagues accompanied her to San Jose to shoot *Steelyard Blues,* in which she portrayed another prostitute. Her funds were running low, and the once big box-office star was living very modestly. "All I need for my current life is a plane ticket, two pairs of jeans, and two sweaters," she said cheerfully. She had given up the movie-star trip and gave fewer and fewer movie-oriented interviews.

61

Jane Fonda, husband Tom Hayden, and children Vanessa and Troy attending the 1980 Academy Awards ceremonies (Fonda was nominated—the fifth time—for The China Syndrome).

She preferred to publish her own statements in the *New York Times* magazine; among other things, she declared, "I will never be a wife again." She explained her relationship with Sutherland:

> We are friends. We think the same things. When we're together it's delightful. When we are apart we remain friends. He is not indispensable to me; I am not indispensable to him. Our attraction involves learning and respect, and we don't expect our relationship to continue forever.

Indeed, the romance faded soon after they completed their third film collaboration. Fonda flew to Paris to begin working with New Wave director Jean-Luc Godard on *Tout Va Bien* ("Everything's All Right"), co-starring Yves Montand. She told French journalists, "They ask, 'Where's her sense of humor?' I haven't lost my humor at all. But it's hard to feel any humor when our bombs are killing innocent Vietnamese." *Tout Va Bien*'s subject matter was the Paris student revolts and strikes of 1968; the actress was following her commitment to making politically conscious films. Unfortunately, such films didn't succeed at the box office.

In Paris she contacted North Vietnamese representatives and expressed a wish to visit their country after attending the 1972 Academy Awards ceremony. She had earlier planned to decline the Oscar if she won, but in her own words,

> A woman who is much wiser than I am said to me, "You're a very subjective individual, an elite individual. The Oscar is what the working class relates to when it thinks of people in the movies. It's important for those of us who speak out for social change to get that kind of acclaim."

Her first victory and her restrained acceptance speech are now part of Hollywood history. A friend and director opined,

> Jane showed what she was made of. It was a beautiful piece of political theater, what she did,

and the next day she could call all those producers and movie moguls up and raise more money than she'd raised in the past two years, just because they were so grateful she didn't screw up their happy little gathering.

Shortly before Oscar, she'd met Tom Hayden. They experienced instant rapport, and when she mentioned that she hoped to visit North Vietnam he proceeded to help. In mid-July she was in Hanoi incognito, but the news of her trip leaked out, and the media had a field day. When she returned she claimed that most of the coverage had been biased and distorted. She had nonetheless incurred the wrath of millions and was greeted in New York by mobs calling her everything from Commie slut to Hanoi Jane. Two Republican congressmen, one running for reelection, branded her a traitor, to which she replied, "What is a traitor? I cried every day I was in Vietnam. I cried for America. The bombs are falling on Vietnam, but it is an *American* tragedy."

At several colleges and antiwar rallies she undertook to explain what she had seen in North Vietnam. When she spoke she was often on the verge of tears. No longer was she an amateur activist. She had laid her career, her reputation, and even her life on the line. Though she received dozens of death threats wherever she went, she would not be silenced. To a reporter who asked if she weren't letting herself be used for propaganda, she retorted,

> Do you think the Vietnamese blow up their own hospitals? Are they bombing their own dikes? Are they mutilating their own women and children in order to impress me? Anyone who speaks out against this war is carrying on propaganda—propaganda for peace, propaganda against death, propaganda for life.

A friend described her anguish as that of "a mother who had lost her child." He claimed,

> The public outcry against her was a sad commentary on the intelligence of the majority . . . those who imagined themselves vigorous defenders of America's honor and integrity. Their

rage was laden with contradictions. . . . The outcry against Jane proved that self-righteousness is still mankind's primary trait and that the concern for plain, objective righteousness is still far beyond our reach, no matter how much lip service we pay to the concept.

Another of the actress-activist's objectives was to bolster the McGovern presidential campaign, but after months of campaigning, the elections yielded a landslide for Nixon. Disheartened, she left for Norway to do a new movie version of the feminist classic *A Doll's House* for celebrated director Joseph Losey, himself a feminist of sorts.

Meanwhile, her relationship with Hayden blossomed, and from Roeros, Norway, they announced their intention to marry. They returned to the United States after the faded star's thirty-fifth birthday. She obtained an overnight divorce from Roger Vadim in the Dominican Republic, and on January 21, 1973, Tom and Jane were wed in Los Angeles in a free-form ceremony attended by about a hundred people, including her family and an assembly of Vietnamese students.

Richard York, the minister who married them, received a "Letter of Godly Admonition" from California's Episcopal bishop two days later, suspending him from further religious duties for "marrying a divorced woman without permission from the bishop."

After her marriage, as the antiwar movement evaporated, Fonda seemed to disappear from public life. She gave birth to Troy O'Donovan Garity on July 7, 1973, and retired into semiconventional motherhood. For three years she led a comfortable, if unluxurious life in Santa Monica.

In 1976 Hayden ran in the California primary for senator against incumbent Democrat John Tunney, a Kennedy look-alike and former political darling. Fonda contributed three-hundred-thousand dollars and countless political speeches to the well-staged campaign. Hayden lost the primary but did far better than expected, prompting him to predict that he would run again.

The couple had already formed a grass-roots organization called the Campaign for Economic Democracy (CED), whose aims were: (1) getting Hayden elected, eventually, to office; (2) lobbying for legislation on behalf of solar energy and investing in SolarCal, which hoped to provide solar-energy technology to California homes by the 1990s; (3) running a five-hundred-thousand-dollar, twelve-acre ranch north of Santa Barbara, which doubled as a summer camp for needy children; and (4) curbing the power of large corporations and monopolies. CED remains one of Fonda's primary concerns, and through it she has become involved with newer issues like the ERA, antinuclear protests, rent control, and secretaries' job rights, as well as statewide and local politics.

Asked how she fits so many roles and activities into her life, she answered,

> By not mingling with the social set in Beverly Hills. That is time wasting. Once I'm finished working for the day I go home and we close the doors. Tom and I discuss projects for the future, and the children are never made to feel separate.

In 1975 she went to the Soviet Union to do a cameo role in the expensive Soviet-American feature *The Bluebird*, starring Elizabeth Taylor. Fonda played the part of Night in a monumental international flop, her last bomb, perhaps the commercial low point of her career.

1976 marked the rebirth of a once-busy, once-commercially viable career. For her comeback she chose the hilarious *Fun with Dick and Jane* to "show people that I can still look pretty and still have a sense of humor." She explained,

> This movie isn't one of your heavy dramas, and I'll admit my role wasn't a big challenge, but it reflects a lot of what's happening in our society. Here is this affluent couple living beyond their means. Then the father's job is pulled out from under him. . . .

It was a topic many could identify with, and it was a hit, reinstating Fonda as big box office.

64

Jane Fonda and son Troy walking in their hometow Santa Monica, California. (Jane sports a Bonnie Raitt–No Nukes T-shirt.)

Audiences found her likable again, and she displayed her best comedic flair in years.

Then came a far more qualitative triumph, *Julia,* based on a chapter from Lillian Hellman's book *Pentimento.* The picture was shot abroad, and Jane had to reaccustom herself to life on her own.

> I've found being on my own strengthens me and keeps me on my toes. My commitment to my family and the causes I believe in is stronger, and this makes me a better actress. I can put everything into my characterization and give the movie my undivided attention. *Julia* means more to me than any movie I've ever made. It's been nothing short of professional ecstasy.

The teaming of Fonda and Vanessa Redgrave worked beautifully, and before the film was completed word got out that veteran director Fred Zinnemann had a masterpiece on his hands and that Jane might receive a second Oscar for it. One of the most publicized films of the seventies, *Julia* heralded a new wave of American movies about women, some pairing actresses the way recent buddy pictures had teamed male stars like Newman and Redford. Fonda did indeed earn an Oscar nomination but lost the award to Diane Keaton, and Redgrave picked up a supporting Oscar for the title role.

The newly busy Fonda told the press,

> Back in the fifties women had to be sexy or glamorous. Women weren't like a James Dean, a Montgomery Clift, or a Marlon Brando, who said, "Screw that stereotype—I'm going to be what I am." Today I'm firmer than ever in my resolve to do only worthwhile, serious films.

After *Julia* she segued into *Coming Home,* her first truly personal project. In the early seventies she had engaged Nancy Dowd to write a screenplay about the Vietnam war's effects on veterans and others. The project evolved over the years, going through several stages, and it was a risky gamble that paid off, the first major movie about a once-unpopular subject. *Coming Home* didn't break box-office records, but it did very well for a "serious" film. It showered pres-

tige and profits on the participants, touched millions of people, and won Jane a second Oscar and Hollywood's unreserved blessings. Her success with her role, and the picture's warm acceptance by all segments of the public, even hawkish vets, were partly due to her restraint:

> All we wanted to do in the movie is to show this woman moving from point A to point B. That's all. It would have been phony to have her undergo some great liberal conversion. Remember, this was 1968, Nixon was in the White House, and it wasn't too easy to be against the war.

The fourth consecutive effort of her big comeback (actually more than that, for she had never been the number-one female superstar) was *Comes a Horseman,* a "different kind of western." Said plain-Jane (she was a weatherbeaten ranchwoman), "It's about a woman and a man who want nothing more than to own a piece of land and be left alone. But they end up fighting large-land holders and oil companies." Another role to sink her teeth into.

During the location shooting, she even made friends with some local cowboys and roughnecks. Later, while she was filming *The China Syndrome,* gay journalist Arthur Bell asked her whether she'd got any negative feedback from such males over her gay-rights stand.

She answered,

> Yes, from cowboys. When I was doing *Comes a Horseman* a few of them would say, "So you're out there with the gays, eh?" It's difficult to answer them, and I have to think. . . . But it doesn't go unnoticed by me that they like to spend time with the boys. And it doesn't go unnoticed that these same men can't understand that I have three black people working for me. You can only hope that they'll like you and listen to you and one day question their own beliefs.

The China Syndrome became her biggest hit ever. It was a commercial presentation of her IPC Films, whose initial effort was a Vietnam documentary titled *Introduction to the Enemy.*

Syndrome was in part the result of her desire to film the story of the late Karen Silkwood,* but Fonda could not obtain motion-picture rights, so she drifted into a nuclear-themed production headed by Michael Douglas. Richard Dreyfuss had backed out of his role as the TV news reporter who pushes the nuclear news story, the role that Jane assumed. Of course, although it was a superb thriller and had a timely topic, *The China Syndrome* became a phenomenon because of the accident at Three Mile Island, which occurred within days after the movie's opening.

Despite a sprained ankle incurred while shooting a *Syndrome* scene on a rocky hillside in high-heeled wedgies, the superstar said enthusiastically, "Now that I'm making movies again I don't think I'll ever want to take off as much time as I did before." She also said, "I may have been a bit shrill in the past, but I've reached the conclusion that rallies and speeches aren't necessarily as effective as making one hell of a good movie!"

Before taking a well-deserved break from nonstop working, she teamed with Robert Redford for the third time, in the commercially oriented message western *The Electric Horseman.* She was again directed by Sydney Pollack (*They Shoot Horses, Don't They?*). Pollack summed up the plot: "The Marlboro Man meets Barbara Walters." Filming took place in Las Vegas casinos and rugged Saint George, Utah. An unexpected blizzard in Saint George in February 1979 caused a two-week delay in filming. Fonda used the hiatus to distribute leaflets on behalf of Los Angeles Working Women and to plan her next film, *Nine to Five,* with Lily Tomlin and Dolly Parton—another popular comedy underlined by a social message, this time about secretaries. Later, in San Francisco, she kicked off National Secretaries Week by leading a rally on fair-employment issues.

After the release of *The China Syndrome,* Fonda made headlines speaking at various antinuke rallies, including a behemoth in Washington, D.C., with California Governor Jerry Brown, who'd previously appointed Tom Hayden to the SolarCal Council. Jane's appointment to the state's arts council was far more controversial, at least among conservative state senators. The bad old days were recalled when headlines blared that the state senate had not only rejected the actress-activist but had denounced her on the floor, calling her, among other things, a traitor, without giving her an opportunity to defend herself.

Hollywood denounced the action, which was reminiscent of the McCarthy era, and the Screen Actors Guild, headed by its president, Jeanette Nolan, took a full-page ad in *Variety* supporting Jane Fonda. Alan Alda revealed on Phil Donohue's TV show that he'd been invited to speak at a University of California campus but that after discovering that Jane's name had been removed from a list of potential speakers because she was

---

Editor's note: For those not familiar with the case, the following brief summary is in order.

In 1972, twenty-six-year-old Karen Silkwood went to work as a nuclear laboratory technician for the Kerr-McGee Corporation (K-M) plant near Oklahoma City that manufactured plutonium rods used in nuclear reactors. Discovering an enormous number of safety hazards at the plant, Silkwood joined the Oil, Chemical and Atomic Workers Union (OCAW), which was attempting to get K-M to comply with safety standards. Silkwood eventually won a seat on the union's three-member steering committee.

In early fall of 1974, Silkwood and the other steering-committee members went to Washington, D.C., to document charges against K-M before the Atomic Energy Commission. Among the documented charges was evidence that seventy-three K-M workers had been internally contaminated with plutonium and dozens of others had been externally contaminated.

On November 5, 1974, Silkwood discovered that she had been contaminated with plutonium, and a subsequent search showed that her entire home had been mysteriously contaminated, with the highest levels being found in food in her refrigerator!

Silkwood had been gathering evidence against K-M, and she made an appointment to deliver a bulky file of documents to Steve Wodka of OCAW and Dave Burnham of the *New York Times* on the evening of November 13, 1974. While she was on her way to the appointment, her car went off the road, and she was killed. (Later investigation showed that another vehicle had forced her car off the road.) Among the first people at the scene of the "accident" were K-M officials. The documentation Silkwood had been delivering disappeared from the scene and has never resurfaced.

Director Colin Higgins confers with Lily Tomlin, Dolly Parton, and Fonda on the set of Nine to Five.

"controversial," he had insisted that his name be removed also.

Summer 1979 found Jane and Tom touring fifty-two American cities on behalf of the CED, focusing on the dangers of nuclear power plants, exorbitant oil-company profits, lack of affordable housing, unemployment, and other vital issues. Back in Los Angeles, she invested approximately a hundred thousand dollars in Jane Fonda's Workout, an exercise-and-dance studio that catered mainly to working women in a "rundown" section of Beverly Hills. Organized by exercise teacher Leni Cazden, and situated in a renovated office building, Jane Fonda's Workout became the site of inexpensive daytime classes including a noontime special that combined exercise, shower, and lunch into a sixty-minute session. "I've been looking for positive ways to invest my money," Fonda stated. "If this place only catered to the Beverly Hills limousine set it would be contradictory." Profits go to Jane and the CED.

The highly paid star had long since ruled out investing in stocks of companies that pollute, discriminate, manufacture weapons, do business with South Africa, or produce products like cigarettes and liquor. (A future investment possibility is the national franchising of Jane Fonda's Workouts, since the original has been such a success.) In spite of a liberal image, Fonda does not shy away from a puritanical label. She told *Playgirl* magazine,

> *Puritanical* may have a negative connotation to it, but I consider it healthy. For example, when jokes were going around Hollywood about Roman Polanski and that thirteen-year-old girl, people were laughing and saying thirteen is *really old*. I don't even know what the jokes were. I just wanted to pretend that I didn't have anything to do with this industry.
>
> I found it shocking and extremely disturbing. And I would never go to a place like Studio 54. It just rubs against every puritanical fiber in my body. I can just *feel* the drugs in there.

Jane began 1980 with *Nine to Five*, followed by *On Golden Pond*, with Henry Fonda and Kath-

arine Hepburn. For an upcoming film in which she plays a jail warden, she will receive the record (for a female star) sum of two million dollars, plus a percentage.

Another Hayden senatorial bid is a distinct possibility in the near future, and as usual, Fonda would staunchly support her husband. Sooner or later, it's possible that among her other achievements, Jane may become a senator's wife (as happened to Liz Taylor). But the actress has stated that in the early eighties she will put politics on the back burner and concentrate on her strong suit: acting. At forty-three, she is at the peak of her powers, but it is anyone's guess how much longer she will be able to attract the choicest roles and most noteworthy projects. At an age when most actresses find their star power diminishing and their salaries shrinking, Jane Fonda is bigger and better than ever, more in demand, and certainly more admired and respected. Although her films invariably contain a message and/or a strong female protagonist, they do very well at the box office, a fact that has not gone unnoticed in Hollywood and may bode better things for women *and* men in the movies . . . and at the movies.

Presenting a 1980 Gold Record to hit singer Michael Jackson.

Tall Story

Warner Bros., 1960. Produced and directed by Joshua Logan. Screenplay by J. J. Epstein, based on the play by Howard Lindsay and Russel Crouse and the novel The Homecoming Game, *by Howard Nemerov.*
PRINCIPAL CAST: Jane Fonda, Anthony Perkins, Ray Walston, Marc Connelly, Anne Jackson, Murray Hamilton, Tom Laughlin.

JANE FONDA'S "unofficial godfather," Joshua Logan (the man behind *South Pacific*), was the first person to direct her in a film. *Tall Story* was a piece of romantic fluff aimed at younger audiences, the story of a brainy coed whose sole reason for attending a particular college is to pursue the star basketball player, portrayed with diligent earnestness by Anthony Perkins, who starred in the unforgettable *Psycho* around the same time.

Girl meets boy, girl gets boy, and girl marries boy. It was perhaps significant that in her very

first screen role, it was Jane who took the initiative, sought a goal, and attained it. However, for all her girlish aggressiveness as June Ryder, she now seems practically prehistoric in the badly dated *Tall Story*. The frantic, juvenile movie is notable now and was notable then only because it introduced Jane Fonda to moviegoers—an inauspicious but colorful start for an amazing screen career.

Jane was a star in her first movie, with star billing and star treatment. Most of this could be attributed to the importance of her father and

Jane Fonda enrolls in a university to be nearer to the object of her affections, Anthony Perkins.

College students Jane Fonda and Anthony Perkins encounter an unsuspecting friend of Perkins.

Fonda and Perkins seek advice from man of the world Tom Laughlin.

his connections and part to her youthful beauty and striking personality. The newcomer radiated innocence and sexiness with equal ease. Her first movie contract was engineered by experts, and though a beginner, she was treated gingerly on the set. The Fonda connection made her especially interesting to both Hollywood and Middle America, but had Jane not been able to deliver star quality or a modicum of talent, it is doubtful she'd have received a second chance.

Critics panned *Tall Story* but were typically impressed by the effervescent female star. She took this praise to heart and stayed away from movies for nearly two years, turning down unworthy offers and improving her craft in the theater. Obviously, Jane Fonda was here to stay.

REVIEWS:

Ellen Fitzpatrick, *Films in Review:* The picture wouldn't be reviewed in these pages but for the fact that Henry Fonda's daughter Jane makes her screen debut in it. She is a good-looking lass and she can act. . . . There are a few moments in this picture when in Miss Fonda's eyes it is possible to see the lineaments of her father. Such moments are rare on the screen and rare in film history.

Time: Nothing could possibly save the picture, not even the painfully personable Perkins doing his famous awkward act, not even a second-generation Fonda with a smile like her father's and legs like a chorus girl. The lines (*"beget*—isn't that a sweet word for it?"*) are stupefyingly cute, the sight gags frantically unfunny, the climax about as exciting as a soggy sweatsock.

Motion Picture: An old-fashioned tale of a man-mad girl, played by cinematic newcomer Jane Fonda, who is unlikely to follow in her father's distinguished footsteps if *Tall Story* is the type of material she will pursue. Still, one must give her credit for trying, and she does manage to turn her shallow, misguided character into a likable, bubbly coed. Anthony Perkins is the perfect foil for Miss Fonda in this gooey, gaudy

Co-ed Jane Fonda eventually traps basketball star Anthony Perkins into love and marriage.

romance. But in comparison with youthful love stories like *A Summer Place* and *Blue Denim, Tall Story* is hopelessly outdated and unrealistic, if harmless.

Howard Thompson, *New York Times:* . . . a frantic attempt at sophistication and a steady barrage of jazzy wisecracks, most of them pretty stale, about campus sex and the business of education. . . . On the court, the gangly Mr. Perkins jounces around convincingly enough. Near Miss Fonda, he generally gapes and freezes, and who can blame him? If Miss Fonda seems to be looking a bit askance now and then, who can blame her?

College students Fonda and Perkins find driving to school a less-than-academic pursuit in Joshua Logan's "super-saucy" comedy Tall Story.

Jane Fonda finds Anthony Perkins's company more fascinating than the lecture by her professor, played by Ray Walston.

Walk on the Wild Side

Columbia, 1962. Directed by Edward Dmytryk. Produced by Charles K. Feldman. Screenplay by John Fante and Edmund Morris, based on the novel by Nelson Algren.
PRINCIPAL CAST: *Laurence Harvey, Capucine, Jane Fonda, Anne Baxter, Barbara Stanwyck.*

NELSON ALGREN had written a sensationalistic novel, very daring at the time, about a young Texan who searches for the girl he left behind. He unexpectedly finds her in a bordello presided over by a Lesbian madame. Kitty Twist is a bratty and amoral hell-raiser who winds up working in the place. The film soft-pedaled the madame's sexual preference but retained the book's sensationalism, turning *Walk on the Wild Side* into an "adult" drama with overriding commercial expectations.

Britisher Laurence Harvey was inexplicably cast as the Texan, which might not have been the case had he not starred in the Oscar-winning *Room at the Top* (with Simone Signoret, Best Actress winner). Many domestic actors of stature were afraid to accept such a controversial role, but Harvey pulled it off with a convincing

Jane Fonda essays the languorous Kitty Twist, a pretty thief and hellraiser.

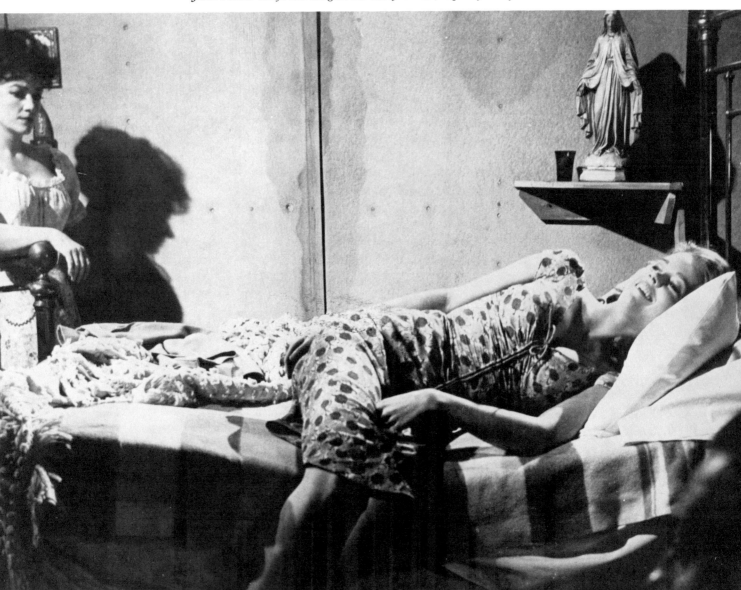

Jane Fonda becomes infatuated with Laurence Harvey, as the Texan who enters her sleazy world.

accent. Jane Fonda stole the show as the rollicking, deliciously bad Kitty Twist, and Barbara Stanwyck essayed the maternal madame. Capucine played the girlfriend turned hooker.

Harvey found Fonda a pleasure to work with. "She's a quick study and an intelligent girl. I understand this is only her second picture, but she's learned more than most actresses who've made half a dozen pictures. She's attractive but not overly concerned with her looks, and she's easy to get along with, though she seems uncomfortable with touching or displays of affection. . . . She *knows* she's sexy, and she also knows when to turn it off."

The past was still very much with Jane, however, and one of her few problems making *Walk on the Wild Side* existed because Stanwyck was an old family friend who had known Jane through most of her childhood and still called her by the nickname Lady Jane. Fonda found she had trouble doing a certain scene with Stanwyck in which she was called upon to act especially trashy. "I just couldn't do it in front of Barbara Stanwyck," she said. She tried several times, and finally a new method of doing the scene had to be found. Many years later, Jane sighed, "It was an example of my past confronting my newer self, and in such confrontations, the past usually wins."

She was plenty sexy and slatternly enough, though. Fonda was the highlight of the much publicized, controversial film. She was well on her way to becoming both an all-American sexpot and a star of considerable talent. One would hardly have thought so at the time, but *Walk on the Wild Side* was a step in the right direction.

79

Jane knew what she was doing: "Kitty Twist is a wonderful acting part—a tough young girl who ran away from an orphanage and reform school and had to steal to survive. She's like a cat, ends up ratting on everybody and getting everybody killed. I never would have thought anyone would offer me this kind of part. I've always been wanted for the ingenue, the girl next door." Her second screen role could hardly have contrasted more with her first.

REVIEWS:

Paul V. Beckley, *New York Herald Tribune:* The movie has oversimplified and overstated Algren's novel. The characters seem pretentious, overdone, leading one to take them too seriously on the one hand and not seriously enough on the other. The compassion, the sense of personal waste that could make the film unusual and penetrating instead of usual and paltry, is crowded out by the constant underlining, the strain for violent emphasis, the insistence on vulgarity rather than precise definition. . . . It is not the actor who is at fault here. Laurence Harvey plays the Texan with more authenticity than one might expect. Capucine, in addition to her natural elegance, here uncovers an infinite capacity for languorous intensity. Jane Fonda, as a bouncy, wiggly, bratty little thief and prostitute, seems more like a Nelson Algren character than anyone else in the picture.

Cinemundo: Walk on the Wild Side is a rare adult drama with a multi-star international cast. . . . The most riveting performance belongs to Miss Stanwyck, as a discreetly lesbian brothel owner with a desire for Miss Fonda, whose second film this is. In her first, forgettable film, she played a naïve student coping with college. In *Walk on the Wild Side,* she graduates to playing a woman who must cope with love, life and her twisted fate. . . . Laurence Harvey, of *Room at the Top* fame, is also outstanding as an American Southerner.

Eventually, Jane Fonda falls in love with Laurence Harvey.

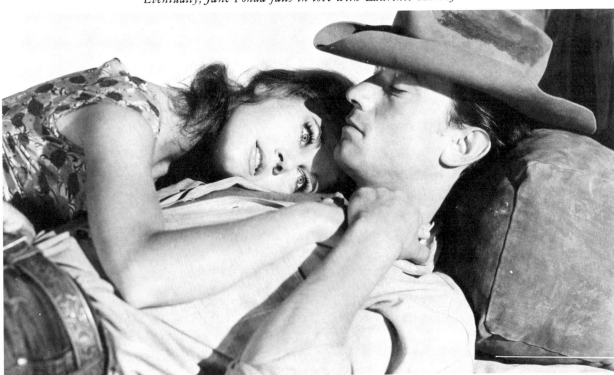

Bosley Crowther, *New York Times:* The prostitute-with-a-heart-of-gold staggers through *Walk on the Wild Side* and has no more substantiality in this instance than she had in the works of the old dime novelists. . . . Everything in this sluggish picture . . . from a novel by Nelson Algren (which it doesn't resemble in the least) smacks of sentimentality and social naïveté. It is incredible that anything so foolish would be made in this day and age. And the suggestions in ads and awesome press releases that there is something "adult" about it, that it is a little too strong for the kids, are sheer, unadulterated eyewash. It's as naughty as a cornsilk cigarette. There is ever so slight a suggestion that the prostitute is admired by the madame of the bordello. But that this is any more than the admiration of an employer for a highly productive employee is a thing that only the most susceptible to press-agentry might suspect.

As the heroine, the tall, thin actress who calls herself Capucine is as crystalline and icy as her elegant mononym. Laurence Harvey is barely one-dimensional and Barbara Stanwyck is like something out of mothballs. Jane Fonda is elaborately saucy and shrill (a poor exposure for a highly touted talent) and Anne Baxter is wasted in a weak role. Edward Dmytryk's direction makes you wonder whether he read the script before he started shooting.

Stanley Kauffman, *The New Republic.* A new talent is rising—Jane Fonda. Her light is hardly under a bushel, but as far as adequate appreciation is concerned, she might as well be another Sandra Dee. I have now seen Miss Fonda in three films. In all of them she gives performances that are not only fundamentally different from one another but are conceived without acting cliché, and executed with skill. Through them all can be heard, figuratively, the hum of that magnetism without which acting intelligence and technique are admirable but uncompelling. . . . In *The Chapman Report* . . . she plays a frigid young middle-class widow. The girl's pathological fear of sex, exacerbated by her hunger for love, is expressed in neurotic outbursts that cut to the emotional quick, with a truth too good for the material.

Fonda and Harvey head for New Orleans.

It would be unfair to Miss Fonda and the reader to skimp her sex appeal. Not conventionally pretty, she has the kind of blunt startling features and generous mouth that can be charged with passion, or the cartoon of passion, as she chooses. Her slim, tall figure has thoroughbred gawky grace. Her voice is attractive and versatile. Her ear for inflections is secure. What lies ahead of this gifted and appealing young actress? With good parts in good plays and films she could develop into a first-rate artist. Meanwhile, it would be a pity if her gifts were not fully appreciated in these lesser, though large, roles.

Cinemundo: The subject of this film stirred up much controversy in the United States, less in Europe. The women's "sexual problems" studied by the research team are relatively tame and almost boring. The director, George Cukor, and the writers have tried to hide the thinness of the plot by intercutting several stories and characters, who have nothing in common but sex and the Chapman Report. It is poor and sensationalistic material for a film with so many talents on both sides of the camera.

Fellow travelers Harvey and Fonda seek a new kind of life together.

The Chapman Report

Warner Bros. 1962. Directed by George Cukor. Produced by Richard D. Zanuck. Screenplay by Wyatt Cooper and Don M. Mankiewicz.
PRINCIPAL CAST: Jane Fonda, Shelley Winters, Claire Bloom, Glynis Johns, Efrem Zimbalist, Jr., Ray Danton, Cloris Leachman, Jack Cassidy.

LIKE *Walk on the Wild Side, The Chapman Report* was based on a sex-sational novel, this one by Irving Wallace. The then ultra-hot topic was a sex-research study, à la Kinsey or Masters and Johnson. The book and movie followed the "personal" (read sexual) lives of four women with four separate sexual hangups, ranging from frigidity to nymphomania. Ironically, Jane Fonda was the frigid one. Handling the largely female cast was the reknowned George Cukor, a so-called women's director responsible for many of Hollywood's greatest films, including Garbo's *Camille, The Women, A Star Is Born* (the Garland version), and several Katharine Hepburn vehicles.

Unfortunately, *The Chapman Report* was not one of Cukor's better efforts. The material was blatantly commercial, promising sex and star-

Jane Fonda as Kathleen Barclay—
a study in frigidity?

83

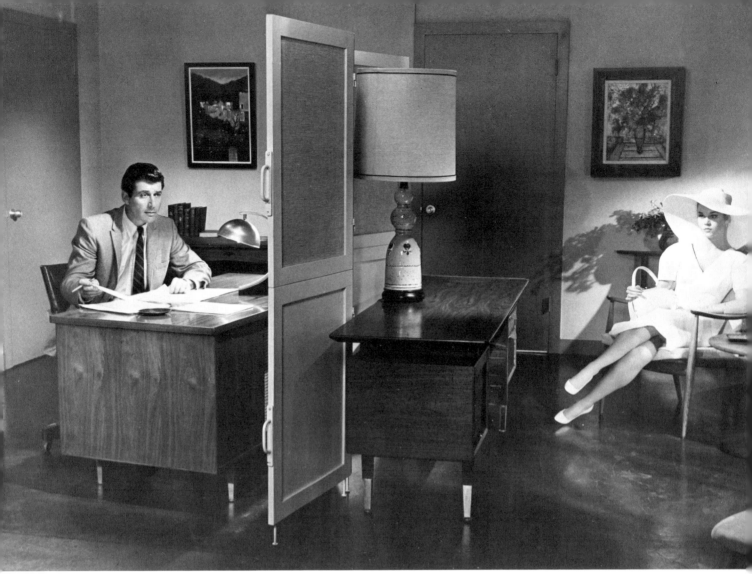

Jane Fonda waits to visit Efrem Zimbalist, Jr., in his office.

tling insights into the four women's lives but delivering only soap opera. When it came out, *Chapman* was deemed adults-only fare; within five years, it was extremely tame, as were its romantic situations.

Jane had originally auditioned for the part of the nymphomaniac, dressed and made up like a streetwalker. Cukor was reportedly amused but saw through to her upper-class, waspish upbringing and cast her as the icy, spoiled young widow with a Connecticut accent. Cukor advised Jane to restrain her natural exuberance before the cameras. Presumably, he had seen *Tall Story* and *Walk on the Wild Side*. He opined, "She has such an abundance of talent that she

must learn to hold it in. She is an American original."

Her reason for seeking the nympho part was that her mentor Andreas Voutsinas had told her that to achieve her full dramatic potential, she must seek out roles heavily shaded with sexuality. After she got the frigid part, she reasoned, "I was disappointed, but it was George Cukor, and you can wait a lifetime to work with him, so I took the part."

Concerning the controversy surrounding her second and third film projects, she felt, "I'm always ready to go out and make a mistake, even though I know I may be criticized. I do it because I'm always thinking my life will be over

84

before I have a chance to do some of these crazy things. For instance, I knew that playing Kitty Twist would make me look very ugly. I thought that my career might be ended because of it, but I went and did it anyway."

The Cukor experience proved worthwhile for Fonda, despite the finished product. She beamed, "There aren't words to describe what it means to work with him. He's a mystical character. . . . He shoots everything fifteen or sixteen times. You know he'll protect you. He has impeccable taste and a sense of subtlety. . . . He's interested in talent. He had me out to his house and told me, 'I've let you do certain things now that if you did them three years from now, I'd knock your teeth in.' He teaches you discipline as an actress."

REVIEWS:

ABC Film Guide: The Chapman Report is a mildly entertaining attempt to cash in on now-fashionable sexual surveys and reports. Leave it to Irving Wallace. . . . Actually, the movie is interestingly cast; the individual performances of the quartet of major actresses are the only compelling reasons to see *The Chapman Report*. . . . Shelley Winters, though increasingly rotund, is nonetheless as good a scene-stealer as ever. Jane Fonda, as a frigid young widow, is more watchable than a clever actress. Glynis Johns and her honeyed voice are quite effective in projecting latent passionate romance, but Miss Bloom, though a proven dramatic performer, is the least interesting of the group. . . . Women's director George Cukor brings a high gloss to the surprisingly bland material.

Jane Fonda at a party with fellow Chapman interviewees Glynis Johns and Shelley Winters.

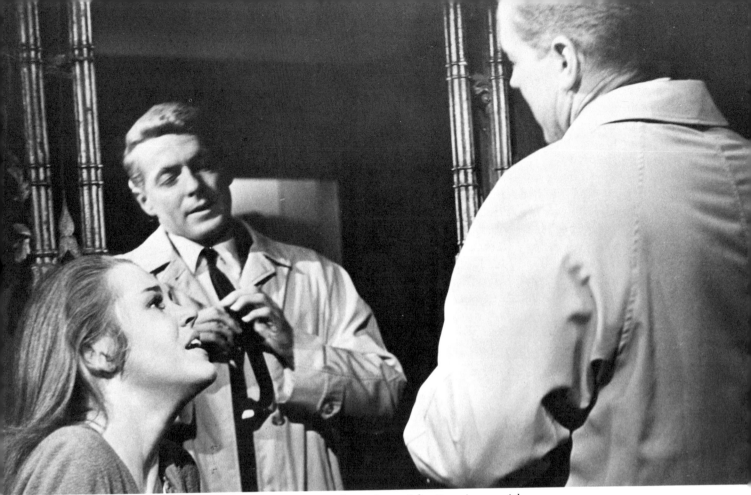

Jane Fonda confronts John Baer in anguish.

Stanley Kauffman, *The New Republic:* A new talent is rising—Jane Fonda. Her light is hardly under a bushel, but as far as adequate appreciation is concerned, she might as well be another Sandra Dee. I have now seen Miss Fonda in three films. In all of them she gives performances that are not only fundamentally different from one another but are conceived without acting cliché, and executed with skill. Through them all can be heard, figuratively, the hum of that magnetism without which acting intelligence and technique are admirable but uncompelling. . . . In *The Chapman Report* . . . she plays a frigid young middle-class widow. The girl's pathological fear of sex, exacerbated by her hunger for love, is expressed in neurotic outbursts that cut to the emotional quick, with a truth too good for the material.

It would be unfair to Miss Fonda and the reader to skimp her sex appeal. Not conventionally pretty, she has the kind of blunt startling features and generous mouth that can be charged with passion, or the cartoon of passion, as she chooses. Her slim, tall figure has thoroughbred gawky grace. Her voice is attractive and versatile. Her ear for inflections is secure. What lies ahead of this gifted and appealing young actress? With good parts in good plays and films she could develop into a first-rate artist. Meanwhile, it would be a pity if her gifts were not fully appreciated in these lesser, though large, roles.

Cinemundo: The subject of this film stirred up much controversy in the United States, less in Europe. The women's "sexual problems" studied by the research team are relatively tame and almost boring. The director, George Cukor, and the writers have tried to hide the thinness of the plot by intercutting several stories and characters, who have nothing in common but sex and the Chapman Report. It is poor and sensationalistic material for a film with so many talents on both sides of the camera.

Fonda and Zimbalist share a tender moment.

Fonda spurns Zimbalist's advice.

Period of Adjustment

MGM, 1962. Directed by George Roy Hill. Produced by Lawrence Weingarten. Screenplay by Isobel Lennart, based on the play by Tennessee Williams.
PRINCIPAL CAST: Jane Fonda, Tony Franciosa, Jim Hutton, Lois Nettleton, John McGiver, Mabel Albertson, Jack Albertson.

THE PERIOD OF ADJUSTMENT of the title refers to crises in two marriages. One such crisis occurs at the start of a jittery marriage between Jane Fonda and Jim Hutton. The other is during an established marriage, on the verge of separation, between Tony Franciosa and Lois Nettleton. After assorted trials and tribulations, the relation- ships are cemented, and all's well that ends well.

It seems incredible that this soporific tale was written by Tennessee Williams. As a Broadway play, it disappointed critics and theatergoers, who expected something like *Cat on a Hot Tin Roof* or *Night of the Iguana.* It fared little better on the screen, but oddly enough, this was

Newlyweds Jane Fonda and Jim Hutton anxiously face the future.

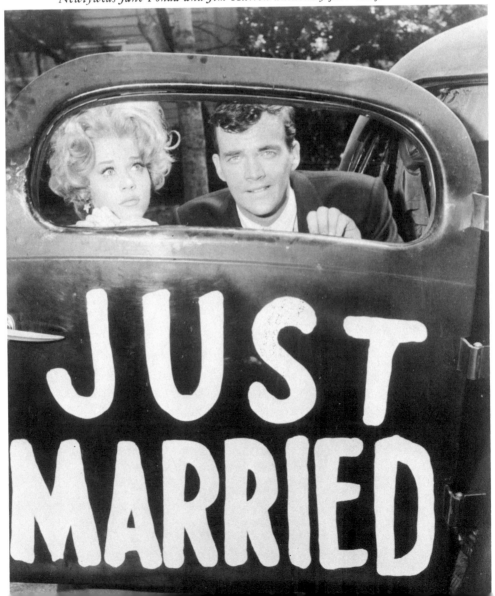

88

Fonda's favorite among her first four films:

> As a bride who cries most of the time throughout *Period of Adjustment,* I don't know how pretty I'll look. The whole story covers a period of twenty-four hours following the wedding, and everything goes wrong. It's a story of the lack of communication between male and female—the old idea that a man must show off his masculinity and a girl must be dainty and weak. They're both so busy living in this framework that they go right past each other.
>
> It was an enormous challenge for me, especially because with my two previous films I felt I'd tried but not gotten a good grasp on the characters I was playing. . . . I became an actress because I needed love and support from a lot of people, but at the beginning I never dreamed I'd end up in the movies. A stage career is what I wanted. But somehow making movies gets to you. It's ego-battering and it's much tougher work, because with all the various things involved it's harder to create a performance. When I did *Adjustment* I finally began to feel like an experienced film actress, and I decided movies were for me.

In her fourth film, Jane's hair was made blond. The Fonda look that reached its height in *Barbarella* (and was shattered by her Vietnam-era shag cut) was taking shape, and she was soon bemoaning the bleached hair, artificial eyelashes, falsies, and cleavage that were becoming part of her appearance, at the insistence of Jack Warner and other movie moguls. Nevertheless, she persisted for some time in playing roles that were racier than those of, say, Natalie Wood and less worthy than, say, Anne Bancroft's. One of her associates declared, "She's marking time—waiting for the right director to come along, take her in hand, and make a real actress of her." As an afterthought he added, "Maybe she should work in Europe."

But Vadim was still two middling movies away, and unfortunately, he didn't fully exploit Fonda's talent but turned her into little more than one of the world's leading sex symbols. Had she become an actress in, say, the Bancroft mold, her later politicization might have come as less of a shock to her public and her motives questioned and criticized less harshly.

Jane Fonda becomes emotional on the day of her wedding (to Jim Hutton).

Newlyweds Fonda and Hutton talk through their problems.

89

REVIEWS:

Bosley Crowther, *New York Times:* Since this is the kind of study in human relationships they know how to make in Hollywood, it is put on and played in proper fashion: much better, we would say, than it was on the Broadway stage. Jane Fonda is appropriately shallow and jittery. Her vague emotions and wispy feelings seem no deeper than her goose pimples which are revealed in some strangely familiar acting. Could it be the late Marilyn Monroe that Miss Fonda seems to resemble? She surely won't mind our saying so. Jim Hutton is apt as her husband, gangling and comical, obviously removed from boyhood by only two or three feet of added height. Tony Franciosa (it used to be Anthony) toils

Fonda reaches the end of her rope in front of Franciosa and Hutton.

*teran married man Tony Franciosa attempts to bol-
 newlywed Jane Fonda's confidence.*

through the role of the six-year husband with charm and authority. A new girl, Lois Nettleton, is sweet as his slightly vapid wife and John McGiver is beautifully crude and snarly as her meanly possessive dad. Isobel Lennart's screenplay adds a few mild embellishments [to the play] and George Roy Hill has directed in a nice, clear, uncomplicated way. The humor and pathos of "adjusting" by clumsy young people is fairly put. The only questions are whether it's worth their efforts and whether it's worth your money to watch them fight.

Time: In 1960, with the sly delight of a cannibal devouring a cookie, shock merchant Tennessee Williams shocked everyone by writing a play about normal people. Well, almost normal . . . The film is favored with the fine young foolishness of Jim Hutton and Jane Fonda, and with one brutal bit of Williamsy whimsey, interpolated by scenarist Isobel Lennart, that catches in a phrase the horror of filial relations in a Spock-marked generation. Only once in the entire film does the father speak in a soothing, amiable tone of voice to his son. "Hello, son," he says. The little boy flinches, glances about guiltily, and then in querulous confusion replies, "I'm not biting my nails."

Stanley Kauffman, *The New Republic:* In Tennessee Williams' comedy, *Period of Adjustment,* which is amusing enough, Jane Fonda plays a nervous Southern bride, anxious in more than one sense. Her comic touch is as sure as her serious one. Besides the gift of timing, she has what lies below all comedy: confidence in one's perception of the humorous—where it begins and especially where it ends. Her performance is full of delights, like the moment when the desolate bride telephones her father long-distance and her tears flood out as she manages to gasp: "Precious Daddy!"

Newlyweds Hutton and Fonda resolve their "period of adjustment" in a romantic manner.

In the Cool of the Day

MGM, 1963. Directed by Robert Stevens. Produced by John Houseman. Screenplay by Meade Roberts, based on the novel by Susan Ertz.
PRINCIPAL CAST: Jane Fonda, Peter Finch, Angela Lansbury, Arthur Hill, Constance Cummings.

1963 PROVED A BAD YEAR professionally for Jane Fonda. In the same year, she did *In the Cool of the Day* for John Houseman (of *Paper Chase* fame) and acted on Broadway in *The Fun Couple,* which lasted all of three performances, despite the pull of the Fonda name. She also terminated her contract with Josh Logan, paying off a hundred thousand dollars to obtain the freedom to do what she wished. With her mentor Andreas Voutsinas, she would go to Greece for a "working holiday."

Complications developed when Voutsinas was informed that if he journeyed to Greece he would be drafted into the Greek army, since he had never done his military service. By then, Fonda had signed, and Houseman insisted she go through with the project, which she was obliged to do, after having her hair dyed brown and shorn into an unappealing banged cut.

It quickly became clear that *In the Cool of the Day* was inferior material, a soap opera in which Jane played a tubercular foreigner in love with British actor Peter Finch and menaced by Angela Lansbury amid spectacular Greek scenery and ruins.

It was a film Fonda would just as soon forget, definitely the low point of a so far undistinguished, if varied, career. It was also an embarrassment for Finch, who went on to such quality fare as *Sunday, Bloody Sunday* and *Network* (which yielded a posthumous Oscar). Many years later he disclosed, "I did the damned film mostly for the money, also for the chance to work with Jane and go to Greece. I accepted too hastily, trusting in the good taste of Mr. Houseman. Romantic soap operettas can sometimes be

Peter Finch and Jane Fonda find love and passion in the cool of the day.

Angela Lansbury, Peter Finch, and Jane Fonda each
ponder their troubled personal lives.

...da and Finch journey to classical Greece, expecting
...vers' holiday.

turned into good trash and please large segments of the public, but *In the Cool of the Day* wasn't even *good* trash."

Finch considered it his worst picture, and perhaps Fonda considers it her worst too.

Back in Manhattan, before appearing in *The Fun Couple,* Jane was chosen by the Defense Department as the year's Miss Army Recruiting. Her acceptance speech, to an audience of officers and recruiters, extolled the virtues of army life and the need for strong, well-prepared troops to discourage the country's enemies.

Jane Fonda is comforted by lover Peter Finch.

REVIEWS:

Cinemundo: Jane Fonda looks plain as a brunette, and Peter Finch is her too-old boyfriend. . . . The only interesting moments occur in a museum inhabited by classical nude statues or amid breathtaking ruins—the ancient ones, not the dissipated stars.

Motion Picture: In the Cool of the Day is a soap opera cliché with lofty ambitions, set in Greece. Miss Fonda is a brunette this time out, and her leading man is the wooden Peter Finch. Most of the characters seem to be sleep-walking, and only Angela Lansbury, an underrated actress, sparks the audience's imagination. Nothing happens in this picture, which is not an inexpensive production, but is merely one part schmaltz, one part travelogue (with stunning backgrounds of Athens' Acropolis) and one part nothingness. Perhaps producer Houseman intended this as the first international soap opera, but don't look for it to be a hit anywhere.

Stanley Kauffman, *The New Republic:* If such matters were legally actionable, Jane Fonda would have grounds for suit against the director Robert Stevens, the screenwriter Meade Roberts, the cinematographer Peter Newbrook and the wardrobe designer Orry-Kelly, each of whom has put her at a disadvantage in her new film, *In the Cool of the Day.* Originally I suppose it was Miss Fonda's fault for having accepted her role in this John Houseman production. Houseman's name is practically synonymous with compromised quality; a producer whose ambitious conscience does not let him rest until, in his commercial pictures, he has tampered with something or someone serious. But once she took the assignment in this glutinous tale, Miss Fonda was then consistently handicapped by all the gentlemen named. One sees her struggling intelligently to give life to the lumber, and one also sees her consistently defeated. None of these matters handicaps Peter Finch, her lover, who is safely asleep throughout.

Love blossoms on the Acropolis for Fonda and Fin

Sunday in New York

MGM–7 Arts, 1964. Directed by Peter Tewksbury. Produced by Everett Freeman. Screenplay by Norman Krasna, based on his play.
PRINCIPAL CAST: *Jane Fonda, Cliff Robertson, Rod Taylor, Robert Culp, Jo Morrow, Jim Backus, Peter Nero.*

Sunday in New York was, of course, filmed in New York City. Fonda's role was a return to the kind of comedy she'd done in *Period of Adjustment* and *Tall Story*. She was trying to avoid heavy-handed disasters like *In the Cool of the Day* and *Walk on the Wild Side*. Comedy, she thought, would make her an actress in the eyes of the public, rather than a misused star. In *Sunday* she played a virgin (as were most unmarried female characters in movies then) who has

Jane Fonda, on her own in New York, quarrels with Rod Taylor.

moved to Manhattan. She is befriended by the proverbial tall, dark, and handsome stranger, and just in the nick of time her protective brother comes along to make sure nothing has happened and nothing will.

Much of *Sunday*'s comedy would now be considered annoyingly coy; one critic mentioned "the obligatory we-were-just-drying-off-in-bathrobes scene." Eileen Tyler spends a good deal of the film explaining to her brother just how innocent the questionable circumstances really are. As in other sex comedies of the early sixties, sex is promised, but only titillation is offered, in miserly portions. By film's end, marriage rears its respectable head, the couple lives happily ever after, and Eileen's brother gets a rest from rushing in and out of that active apartment.

For all its triteness, *Sunday in New York* fared much better at the box office than Fonda's earlier melodramas. Critics dismissed the movie but praised the leading lady, as they had in *Period of Adjustment*. Jane found, "Making the picture was completely fun from start to finish, which is more than I can say for the other films I've made. The part could have been boring, but it wasn't. I'm sure this movie will help my career." It did, and thus far comedy was her forte, but her next effort would be a total departure— to France, where she would learn to provide more than just titillation.

REVIEWS:

Stanley Kauffman, *The New Republic:* Jane Fonda's last film, *In the Cool of the Day,* was an insurmountable disaster, but it does not disprove her emotional powers in *The Chapman Report* or her comic powers in *Period of Adjustment* and this film. Miss Fonda has wit, even when Krasna doesn't. It is in the immediacy of her voice, her readings of lines, her sharp sense of timing. The combination of her slightly coltish movements and her unpretty but attractive face gives her a quality that cuts agreeably across the soft grain of most young actresses. Her presence has the instant incisiveness and interest that are usually summed up in the term "person-

Rod Taylor and Robert Culp encounter each other in Jane Fonda's apartment.

Cliff Robertson introduces Jo Morrow and Jane Fonda.

99

ality." This last is certainly not identical with talent; Alec Guinness has large talent, little personality. Miss Fonda has considerable of both. It is still worth wondering—up to now, anyway—what will become of her.

Motion Picture: Will she or won't she, and if she agrees, will she be saved on time? These are the central questions in this lightweight but sustained "adult" farce. . . . In several of her recent films, Miss Fonda is a consummate tease. Her roles insinuate sex but yield only a knowing wink; now that she has mastered this role, perhaps it is time for her to move on to more challenging stuff. Unlike most of her co-stars, she has the raw material to develop, if she's willing to give it a try.

Time: Another brightly salacious Hollywood

Jane Fonda shares a Japanese dinner with Cliff Robertson, Rod Taylor, and Robert Culp.

comedy about the way of a man with a girl who just may.... As usual, winking wickedness turns out to be merely eyewash, but the plot—more to be pitied than censored—gets a buoyant lift from stars Jane Fonda, Cliff Robertson and Rod Taylor. All three of them abandon themselves to the film version of Norman Krasna's trite Broadway farce, with disarming faith, as though one more glossy, glittering package of pseudo-sex might save the world.... *Sunday* scores on style. Director Peter Tewksbury has caught Manhattan in a mood of after-the-rain freshness, and the gags are all neatly paced and frequently funny. Even the obligatory we-were-just-drying-off-in-bathrobes scene squeaks by—probably because Jane, in a plain blue wrapper, looks so honey-hued and healthy that her most smoldering invitation somehow suggests that all she really has in mind is tennis.

Fonda rows Taylor through Central Park.

Fonda reacts coolly to Taylor's choice of reading matter.

Joy House

MGM, 1964. Directed by René Clement. Produced by Jacques Bar. Screenplay by René Clement, Pascal Jardin, and Charles Williams, based on the novel by Day Keene.
PRINCIPAL CAST: *Alain Delon, Jane Fonda, Lola Albright, Sorrell Booke.*

AFTER COMPLETING *Sunday in New York,* Fonda flew to Paris to star in Clément's *Joy House,* which was partly financed by MGM, then trying to exploit America's obsession with the *nouvelle vague.* Five years earlier, Jane had journeyed to France as an art student studying the language. But this time her arrival on the Continent was orchestrated by public-relations experts who aimed to make her a star in France too. She was a bigger hit than anyone expected, and it didn't hurt that her French was grammatically correct, though alien. She called everyone *thou,* used droll Americanisms, and appeared in revealing outfits, conversing about her famous father, films, sexuality, and her leading man.

"I will undoubtedly fall in love with Alain Delon," she giggled. "I can only play love scenes well when I am in love with my partner." Soon after, Delon broke up with his lover, Romy Schneider, the Austrian actress who was also a French superstar. The publicity mushroomed.

"This time I had a girl linguist with me," said Jane, "and I didn't speak one word of English for two months. And all that publicity, with reporters constantly crowding in—they adore my father in Europe. All this, mind you, in my French. It was wonderful. I never felt so good."

The romance with Delon didn't go far, and she worked hard to get her French right for the film. Unfortunately, *Joy House* came out haphazard at best; she offered, "There was no script and very little organization. It sort of threw me because I'm used to working within a structured framework. There was just too much playing it by ear for my taste. But Clement is still a wonderful director."

With all the publicity and acclaim, it was inevi-

Jane Fonda as the complicated Melinda.

Jane Fonda, serving rations to the poor, first notices Alain Delon.

Jane Fonda, Lola Albright, and Alain Delon depart Albright's French mansion.

table that Jane would get to know still another "wonderful" director, Roger Vadim—the francophile Russian who had molded the sex-oriented careers of Bardot, Stroyberg, and Deneuve. One popular song compared Fonda to a gazelle. She was soon in demand as a cover girl, even for toney publications like *Cahiers du Cinéma,* and she was constantly compared to France's reigning icon, Brigitte Bardot. Writer Georges Belmont rhapsodized, "On the outside, she's true to her image: tall, blonde, the perfect American, with long, flexible movements. Inside she is sultry and dangerous, like a caged animal. . . . I watched her move and thought in a flash of the black panther I used to watch in the zoo." The statement is ironic, in light of Jane's later involvement with America's version of black panthers.

Vadim took up where Delon left off, and had it not been for his intervention, Fonda's career and personal history would likely have been very different. Insiders said she found Alain Delon attractive but dull, for he was no match for her intellectually and was perhaps too young for her taste.

Despite all the hoopla over its leading lady, *Joy House* was a moderate success in France but a failure in the United States, too foreign and garbled for the domestic market. Except for Vadim, Jane might never again have worked in Europe. . . .

Along with other critics, Judith Crist put *Joy House* on her Ten Worst Films List for 1965, with the comment, "Come to think of it, wasn't it in *Joy House* that Jane Fonda or somebody says, 'I broke the Ming—do we glue it together?' "

Joy House, originally titled *Ni Saints, ni Saufs* ("Neither Saints, nor Saviors"), was supposed to be a suspense thriller in the Hitchcock vein but was instead a bizarre mishmash by the famous French director René Clement. The main character was played by France's leading leading man, Alain Delon, as a petty criminal on the run from the underground. On the Riviera, he seeks refuge in a flophouse whose soup line is served

Fonda prepares a meal for handsome house guest Delon.

by Jane Fonda and Lola Albright. The two women move Delon to a Gothic mansion owned by Albright, a millionairess with a Salvation Army complex. Jane, her cousin, is hot for Alain and sleeps in his bed as often as she can—but Delon is usually in bed with Albright, a widow with a mad lover who is roaming the secret corridor that encircles the eerie mansion.

Delon is ill-at-ease, for Albright keeps a shrunken head in a glass case; someone is attempting to poison him; and his murderous former associates have got wind of his whereabouts. Meanwhile, Jane is still trying to get Alain into bed. . . .

REVIEWS:

Judith Crist, *New York Herald Tribune:* Miss Fonda has some mysterious hold over Miss Albright. It's not all Miss Fonda has—or at least so she attempts to indicate by alternately impersonating the Madwoman of Chaillot, Baby Doll and her father Henry; she's a sick kid, this one.

In the attic of the French mansion, Fonda and Alain Delon play with her kitten.

Alain Delon and Jane Fonda share a love-hate relationship in Joy House.

Samedi et Dimanche magazine: *Ni Saints, ni Saufs* is no better, no worse than the recent films of Alain Delon. The major revelation is Jane Fonda, "the American BB," as Melinda. Her French is surprisingly good and her sex appeal is estimable. She has the potential to be a sex symbol in the tradition of Bardot or Monroe, and if she collaborates with Vadim, the results will be interesting.... Fonda is America's gift to Frenchmen.

Cinemundo: The beautiful but macabre mansion is the real star of this movie, which brings American star Jane Fonda, the daughter of Henry Fonda, to the European screen. She is as unlike her widely respected father as a daughter can be. Her function in this movie is purely decorative, and though she is as handsome as Alain Delon, he is better suited to the instinctive direction of René Clement.

Stanley Kauffman, *The New Republic:* The question of Jane Fonda's development into an extraordinarily good actress, which I still think quite possible, is beclouded by her poor choice of vehicles. Her latest film is an absurd suspense picture called *Joy House,* in which Lola Albright and that talented character actor, Sorrell Booke, are also mired. No summary of the silly plot is needed.

Circle of Love

Walter Reade–Sterling, 1965. Directed by Roger Vadim. Produced by Robert and Raymond Hakim. Screenplay by Jean Anouilh, based on the movie La Ronde, *from the play* Reigen, *by Arthur Schnitzler.*

PRINCIPAL CAST: *Jane Fonda, Marie Dubois, Claude Giraud, Anna Karina, Maurice Ronet, Catherine Spaak, Jean Sorel.*

Circle of Love was a remake of *La Ronde,* a post-war movie classic adapted from a play by Arthur Schnitzler. The original *La Ronde* starred Danielle Darrieux as the Married Woman, with Gerard Philipe, Simone Signoret, Jean-Louis Barrault, Simone Simon, and Anton Walbrook, all major French stars. The revamped story (still called *La Ronde* in the French version) was a sex-

ual comedy of errors that took advantage of the star power of Jane's name on two continents and the permissiveness of the French cinema. Fonda assumed the nameless Darrieux role and did her first semi-nude scene, which created a sensation in the United States.

In New York City a seventy-foot billboard was erected above Broadway, bearing the leg-

Jane Fonda is literally swept off her feet by lover Jean-Claude Brialy in Roger Vadim's titillating Circle of Love—*a French but, alas, not an American, hit.*

Jane Fonda, as the married woman, shares an intimate moment with her older husband, played by Maurice Ronet.

end *"Circle of Love,* with Jane Fonda" and featuring a gigantic blond Jane lying belly-down on a rumpled bed, her back and buttocks fully exposed. She and her family were mortified by the painted billboard, and she threatened to sue over the unauthorized picture, which was then altered to cover the Fonda derriere, then taken down completely.

Jane and her director got along famously; he took to calling her Kiki, and she called him Vadim, which was really a diminutive of his middle name. Fonda was well liked in France, and her charm flowed easily. Even Bardot liked "the American Bardot." Jane soon fell in love with Vadim. She explains,

> I met Vadim that first time in Paris when I went to study painting. I heard things about him

then that would curl your hair. That he was sadistic, vicious, cynical, perverted, that he was a manipulator of women.

> Then I saw him again in Hollywood a couple of years later, and he asked me to meet him for a drink to talk about doing a picture. I went, but I was terrified. Like, I thought he was going to rape me there in the Polo Lounge. But he was terribly quiet and polite. I thought, "Boy, what a clever act." Then, back in Paris the second time, he wanted to talk to me about doing *La Ronde.* Okay, I'm older and I think, "I never gave the guy a chance." This time—well, I was absolutely floored. He was the antithesis of what I'd been told.

Making the movie was traumatic for her at first, and Vadim has said that her personal barriers were "as high as the Great Wall of China."

109

Fonda put it this way: "I began making the film, and I fell in love with him. I was terrified. I thought, 'My God, he's going to roll over me like a bulldozer. . . . I'll be destroyed. My heart will be cut out, but I've got to do it.' And I discovered a very gentle man. So many men in America are . . . *men*-men, always having to prove their strength and masculinity. Vadim was not afraid to be vulnerable—even feminine, in a way. And I was terrified of being vulnerable."

The atmosphere on the movie's set may have had something to do with the romance between actress and director; she spent most of her acting time in bed with either the husband or the lover of the character she portrayed. In real life, Fonda moved into a seventeenth-century luxury apartment on the rue Seguier, on the banks of the Seine. Vadim soon joined her, and the French press had a field day that culminated when the two got married.

After completing the English soundtrack for *Circle of Love* (the film was shot in French, with Vadim coaching Jane in her accent), the newlyweds traveled for the first time to the Soviet Union, land of Vadim-Plemiannikov's ancestors. It proved an eye-opening experience for the American.

"I couldn't believe it," she said on her return. "All my life I'd been brought up to believe the Russians were some alien, hostile people sitting over there just waiting to swallow up America. Nothing could be further from the truth. I was amazed how friendly and kind and helpful they were. My eyes were really opened to the kind of propaganda we've been exposed to in America. Every American should go to Russia to see for himself. They'd have a completely different idea of the people."

When she made similar comments during interviews with American reporters, she was chastized; one angered magazine editor snapped, "Who cares what Jane Fonda thinks about Russia? We did her a favor by keeping that stuff out of print. The American people want to know about her sex life, not how noble she thinks the Russians are. If we printed that stuff she'd turn into box-office poison."

Circle of Love, La Ronde became a hit, but Fonda's biggest successes, as well as the biggest changes, were still ahead of her.

REVIEWS:

London Movie Express: Circle of Love is chiefly noteworthy for Jane Fonda in this remake of *La Ronde,* the French classic of not too long ago. Perhaps our memories of *La Ronde* (inexplicably translated as *Circle of Love* by the American distributor) are too fresh, but Fonda is not Danielle Darrieux, and the rest of the undistinguished cast (save the sloe-eyed Anna Karina) cannot compete with the original, which included Simone Signoret, Gerard Philipe and Simone Simon. Vadim directs with complete mastery over Miss Fonda, who is not bad but is miscast and too American for the story. She has a long way to go before becoming another Bardot, if indeed

After a romantic encounter with Jean-Claude Brialy, married woman Jane Fonda finds herself torn between two loves.

that is her aim. . . . Her clothes are unusual, to say the least, and she seems most natural in bed with the winsome Mr. Brialy.

Eugene Archer, *New York Times:* The dubbed *Circle of Love* . . . [has] nothing to recommend it beyond some attractive color photography by Henri Decae. . . . The only tolerable voice in the collection belongs to Jane Fonda, who uses her own—though it has no relationship to her lip movements, since she played the part in French. Wildly miscast, as the discreet and timid matron, the part Miss Darrieux made hers for life, the improving Miss Fonda plays against type. With some comic skill, she creates a perverse imp who speaks modestly while her gestures and expressions pointedly belie her words. In the film's most diverting episode, Miss Fonda cavorts in bed with Jean-Claude Brialy.

Samedi et Dimanche magazine: In the U.S., where *La Ronde* is all but unknown, the major noise made by *Circle of Love* (the English title) was a mammoth nude billboard in Manhattan, which Mlle. Fonda deemed unflattering for some reason. *Circle of Love* does not stand a comparison with *La Ronde,* but on its own terms it is one of Vadim's more engrossing recent movies, and Jane Fonda, America's gift to France in her last vehicle (*Joy House*), may be the next actress Vadim molds into a child-woman of universal appeal. . . . He has never before had the opportunity to mold an American, and only time will tell whether this seemingly emancipated woman bends to his will. Fonda's range is greater than earlier Vadim-creations, and she would probably have had a flourishing career even if she had not been born the daughter of Henry Fonda and even if she had never set foot in France.

Jane Fonda returns to the bed of her husband, Maurice Ronet—for a while.

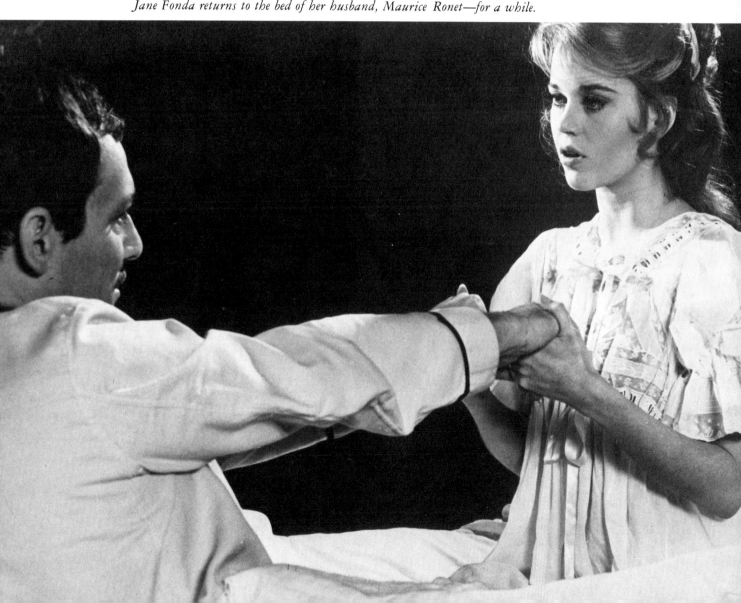

Cat Ballou

Columbia, 1965. Directed by Elliot Silverstein. Produced by Harold Hecht. Screenplay by Walter Newman and Frank R. Pierson, based on the novel by Roy Chanslor.
PRINCIPAL CAST: *Jane Fonda, Lee Marvin, Michael Callan, Dwayne Hickman, Nat King Cole, Stubby Kaye, Tom Nardini, John Marley.*

Cat Ballou was by far Jane Fonda's biggest hit to date, though she had to share the spotlight with Lee Marvin, whose dual good-bad role won him an Academy Award and made him a leading man after years of playing second-string villains. The Cat Ballou of the title was Jane Fonda, as a former schoolmarm who takes up thieving and robbery, hooking up with a gang of amateurs headed by Lee Marvin. *Cat Ballou* was a spoof of westerns, with abundant satire, wit, and even romance. The plot was minimal and the characters cartoon-like, especially Marvin's—in his evil incarnation, he wore an artificial silver nose, and his costume was shiny black leather.

Jane Fonda as Cat Ballou, ingenue turned outlaw.

A large supporting cast added humor, variety, and slapstick to the film, which included the last screen appearance by Nat King Cole, as an old-fashioned balladeer. For Fonda, it was an enjoyable movie to make, and her pleasure showed on the screen. Audiences loved *Cat Ballou*'s irreverence and campiness, and Jane was ebullient, a sexy yet wholesome leading lady. Marvin's Oscar didn't hurt business any, and the film became one of the top grossers of the year.

Cat Ballou was made in California and Colorado, and Fonda took Vadim with her. One of the co-stars remembered, "There we were on location in the hills of Colorado, and here was this Frenchman in horn-rimmed glasses reading *Mad* magazine—all by himself, sitting on a chair on the mountainside while Jane was filming. They weren't standoffish at all. Between scenes, at lunch, they joked around with everyone. Vadim's a very friendly guy."

Though the American press painted a jaded, somewhat decadent picture of Vadim, reveling in often fictitious stories about Fonda's relationship with him, friends who knew the pair had a different impression. One friend from Jane's Actors Studio days revealed, "Jane and Vadim were really in love. He treated her with deference and affection, and she was prouder than a peacock of him. From the stories I'd heard, I expected to walk in on an orgy, and to tell the truth I was a little disappointed to find everything so quiet and domesticated."

The couple was preparing to return to France (before coming back to do *The Chase*) and convert an old French farmhouse in the countryside near Saint-Ouen into their permanent home.

Fonda was now a bona-fide superstar, and comedy obviously suited her and her audiences. But rather than settling into the niche she'd been searching for, once she found it, she determined to give herself new challenges and perfect her skills in dramatic and foreign films as well.

REVIEWS:

Bosley Crowther, *New York Times:* It is a carefree and clever throwing together of three or four solid western stereotypes in a farcical

Dwayne Hickman, Tom Nardini, and Jane Fonda discuss their promising futures.

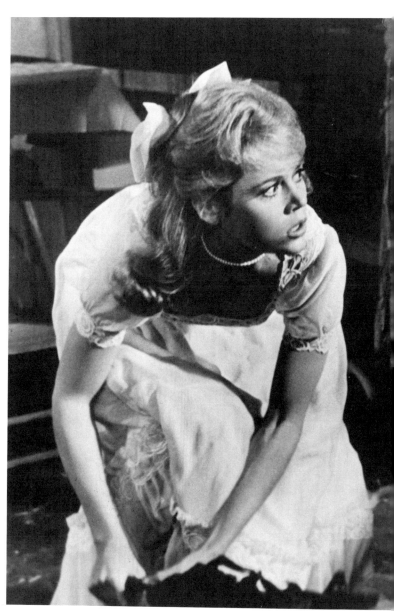

Jane Fonda, as the Cat, is initiated into a merry life of crime.

frolic that follows—and travesties—the ballad form of western story-telling made popular in *High Noon*.... The heroine—Cat Ballou—of Jane Fonda is a big-eyed, big-hearted grown-up child, a veritable Little Mary Sunshine who takes to gunning and robbing a train with the gee-whiz excitement of a youngster confronted with a huge banana split.

Time: As honest-to-gosh westerns go, *Cat Ballou* is disgraceful. As a shibboleth-shattering spoof, it dumps all the heroic traditions of horse opera into a gagbag, shakes thoroughly and pulls out one of the year's jolliest surprises. What's good about the comedy is nigh irresistible.

Jane Fonda, with a little help from a friend, tries to get the better of John Marley.

What's best about it is probably Lee Marvin. Dressed in snaky black, with a silver schnozz tied on where his nose used to be before "it was bit off in a fight," Marvin soberly parodies several hundred western badmen of yore, then surpasses himself as the dime-novel hero, Kid Shelleen.... His eyes are bloodshot from poring over whisky labels. On ceremonial occasions he wears a corset.... Director Elliot Silverstein, freshly sprung from television, sows this wild-oater with all manner of trickery, and most of it works....

In a performance that nails down her reputation as a girl worth singing about, actress Fonda does every preposterous thing demanded of her with a giddy sincerity that is at once beguiling, poignant and hilarious. Wearing widow's weeds over her six-guns, she romps through one of the zaniest train robberies ever filmed, a throwback to Pearl White's perilous heyday. Putting the final touches on a virginal white frock to wear at her own hanging, she somehow suggests that Alice in Wonderland has fallen among blackguards and rather enjoys it. Happily, *Cat Ballou* makes the enjoyment epidemic.

Judith Crist, *New York Herald Tribune:* Well, let's get those old superlatives out again, this time for a small package of enormous delight labeled *Cat Ballou,* a western to end all westerns (or at least our ever looking at another with a straight face) and a comedy that epitomizes the sheer fun of movie-making and movie-watching.

What distinguishes *Cat Ballou* is that in this western nobody is camping, nobody's tongue-in-cheeking and spitballing around. In the title role Jane Fonda is as sweet and pure and earnest as any schoolmarm turned gang leader and man-killer—and it's not her fault that when she slowly canters away astride her horse the one fleeting rear view director Silverstein permits us makes Miss Jane in her riding clothes infinitely sexier than Miss Andress in bikini, ad infinitum. And Lee Marvin—who runs off with the picture and, if there is justice in the contemporary Far West, an Oscar in his dual role of Tim Straun, the silver-nosed evil gunslinger, and Kid Shel-

114

leen, the last alcohol-preserved good gunslinger—doesn't yield by the glitter of an eye as he snarls, as Tim, "If you wasn't a girl I'd split you in two like a chicken," or as Kid, by the blear of a drunkard's eye as he recites a eulogy on the passing of the Day of the Gunfighter. And Stubby Kaye and the late Nat King Cole don't miss a pluck of the banjo or a throb of passion as they appear on screen to punctuate each episode with the ballad to explain what's been happening and why they're hanging Cat Ballou in Wolf City, Wyoming, in 1894.

Pauline Kael, *The New Yorker: Cat Ballou* is the kind of movie which publicity handouts and all too often even reviews describe as zany romps and frolics, the performers as madcaps, piquant and beguiling. But it's uneven, lumpy, coy and obvious, a self-consciously cute movie with so many things thrown into it—many of them over and over again—and with so little consistency or sureness of attitude that I was reminded of an architect friend telling me about the prosperous businessman and his wife who came to see him about building a $100,000 house. "You can do anything you want," they told him, "so long as it doesn't have any style."

Two Lee Marvins—playing bad and good gunfighters—may not suffice; perhaps some in the audience may not appreciate parody, may long for a "real" romance—therefore a younger hero is also provided. Youth is supposed to be so attractive that it doesn't require characterization (which might even be considered a deterrent, limiting possible audience appeal), so Callan just cavorts, grinning archly to convey sexiness. And on the chance that he isn't well known enough, there's Hickman of TV "fame" cavorting, and so on. There are even two minstrels. Wasn't Cole enough? Is it perhaps that Stubby Kaye makes it cuter? A black man and a fat man—so nobody can fail to realize that the ballad singing is "for fun."

It's a spoof, and it spoofs the only safe target—itself. Yet it is so uncertain of its tone that it even tries for a little poignancy or extra depth—something that can pass for meaning or a statement—by having Cat say to the aged robbers who have lost their spirit, "How sad—you got old." It isn't age that's sad, it's wasted lives—like the lives of moviemakers in a commercialized culture who don't know what they want to do or are too fearful to do it. The people who made this movie are in no position to pity others for lacking spirit.

Cat Ballou and her pals: Dwayne Hickman, Michael Callan, John Marley, and Tom Nardini.

The Chase

Columbia, 1966. Directed by Arthur Penn. Produced by Sam Spiegel. Screenplay by Lillian Hellman, based on the novel and play by Horton Foote.

PRINCIPAL CAST: *Marlon Brando, Jane Fonda, Robert Redford, James Fox, Angie Dickinson, E. G. Marshall, Janice Rule, Miriam Hopkins, Martha Hyer, Robert Duvall, Jocelyn Brando.*

The Chase's story, by Lillian Hellman, an infrequent contributor to the screen, was based on characters created by Horton Foote. Unfortunately, the story was the root of this movie's many problems. Basically, the plot is this: Bubber Reeves (Redford) escapes from jail and heads for town, where his wife (Fonda) is having an affair with the son (Fox) of the local bigshot (Marshall). Sheriff Calder (Brando) opposes the town's corrupt forces and tries to save Bubber from being lynched by the townspeople. Various subplots involve the sheriff's wife (Dickin-

Jane Fonda and her lover, James Fox, receive the news that her husband, played by Robert Redford, has escaped from jail and may have murdered a man.

son), some sex-starved local wives, racial bigots, and a mob or two.

After a long, complicated night filled with a large supporting cast, Fonda's lover is killed, Redford is caught by Brando but is murdered by local goons in front of the jailhouse, and the sheriff and his wife, their heads held high, leave town for a new life.

Because of its splendid talents, both in front of and behind the cameras, *The Chase* was a much-anticipated big-budget film. It was produced by the quality-conscious producer of *The Bridge on the River Kwai* and *Lawrence of Arabia.* Sam Spiegel hired Lillian Hellman to fashion a powerful, socially relevant screenplay, and Arthur Penn was signed to direct a cast headed by Brando, Fonda, and the emerging Robert Redford.

However, *The Chase* was no boon to Brando,

who had fallen from both critical and box-office grace; and although this film was the biggest superproduction (in terms of money and co-stars) that Fonda had been involved in, it did little for her, either. Several critics felt she was ill-suited to drama, which she wouldn't completely disprove until *They Shoot Horses, Don't They?*

The filming took almost six months. There was no denying the project's ambitiousness; co-star Redford thought the film suffered from "the kitchen-sink syndrome," trying to do too much with too many characters. He explained, "The hub of the film was centered around four people—the character I played, his wife, the father on the hill [Marshall], and the sheriff. It *was* a chase, but the movie wasn't a chase—it just tried to bring in all the liberal concepts of civil rights."

The Chase wasn't just any flop or failure, and because of its presumptuousness it received an

Jane Fonda and James Fox share a passionate moment before she is contacted by her escapee husband.

In an uncharacteristically light moment, Jane Fonda jokes with Sheriff Marlon Brando, who hopes to capture Robert Redford before he can be harmed by the town's rednecks.

inordinate amount of condemnation and bad reviews. It was one of Columbia Pictures' biggest bombs of the sixties, a movie that most of its stars later disowned.

REVIEWS:

Richard Schickel, *Life: The Chase* is no longer a modest failure. Thanks to the expenditure of a great deal of time, money and talent, it has been transferred into a disaster of awesome proportions. . . . A valiant minority of the star cast—Miss Fonda, Robert Redford, James Fox, Angie Dickinson—try to keep their head while all about them are losing theirs. But their isolated moments of lucidity are no more effective against the fever than cold compresses; they relieve but cannot cure.

Bosley Crowther, *New York Times:* Everything is intensely overheated in *The Chase.* . . . The only thing that is not overheated—at least, I don't think it will be—is the audience's reaction. This is a picture to leave you cold. Yes, it's a phony, tasteless movie, and it is unbelievably played by E. G. Marshall as the town's Mr. Gotrocks, James Fox (the English actor) as his son, Jane Fonda as the trollop wife of the fugitive (who is frying her own kettle of fish with Mr.

*Jane Fonda and lover James Fox find her husband, Robert Redford, hiding out
from the law and angry townspeople in a junkyard.*

Fox), Robert Redford as the homing fugitive and Janice Rule as one of the local lust-filled wives. I should add that it is in garish color, and takes place, street scenes and all, in studio sets.

Judith Crist, *New York Herald Tribune: The* *Chase* is contrivance from beginning to end—a successful contrivance, I am quick to report, a series of shameless clichés and stereotypes balled up with such skill that you roll right along with them to a smashing conclusion. And hate yourself for having been hooked, a half hour later. The big-name performers offer professionalism, too, some with their accomplished polish, some in a manner befitting the stereotypes they are called upon to be.... We end *The Chase* tense, exhausted and frustrated, in sequence. Well, why look back? At worst, you've had a run for your money.

Time: The Chase is a shockworn message film, smoothly overacted and topheavy with subtle bigotry, expertly exploiting the violence, intolerance and mean provincialism that it is supposed to be preaching against. With star Marlon Brando as the chief jeerleader, the movie smugly points an accusing finger at all the wrong, wrong deeds done by precisely the right people.... Miss Hellman seldom lets a scene end without tacking on her comment; except for a handful of courageous, long-suffering Negroes and Sheriff Brando, no Texan escapes being singed by a Statement. Brando ably plays the stereotyped champion of human rights that he seems compelled to endorse in film after film, changing only his dialect. Jane Fonda conquers a casting error as Bubber's faithless wife, making trollopy white trash seem altogether first class.

Jane Fonda discusses a scene with director Arthur Penn, during a break in The Chase.

Rex Reed, *New York Daily News:* Ignoring the fact that such things are completely out of style, out of fashion and out of date, Lillian Hellman has set her screenplay (the term is used loosely, because that is how most of it is written) in the most wife-swappin'est, blackheartedest, gun-totin'est, possum-huntin'est, nigger-hatin'est town in Texas....

The action all takes place in one night that is so badly lit I often had difficulty seeing just who was talking....

There's a lot of talent here, and it should have all stayed home. *The Chase* is the worst thing that has happened to movies since the year Lassie played a war veteran with amnesia.

Any Wednesday

Warner Bros., 1966. Directed by Robert Ellis Miller. Produced and written by Julius J. Epstein, based on the play by Muriel Resnick.
PRINCIPAL CAST: *Jane Fonda, Jason Robards, Dean Jones, Rosemary Murphy, Ann Prentiss.*

Jane Fonda as Ellen Gordon, supported by Rosemary Murphy.

Any Wednesday's plot—about a corporate mistress turning thirty and having to decide between marriage or more of the same—was once daring and controversial. When the play opened on Broadway, little was expected of it, but it created a minor stir and became a surprise hit. A popular Manhattan pastime was speculating which actress would play Ellen Gordon in the movie version. Natalie Wood, Debbie Reynolds, and Audrey Hepburn were all mentioned for the role, but Jane Fonda got it.

Although the film opened up and expanded the claustrophobic play, even adding an urban power blackout, it did little to improve on the original. It had little substance, and any controversy was obviated for the sake of a wider audience. Fonda's wholesome mistress was more akin to an overindulged niece` than a kept woman. There was chemistry between Fonda and Robards, but that chemistry would grow with their stature and talent and was meager in this film, compared to their chemistry in the subsequent *Julia* and *Comes a Horseman.*

By the time *Any Wednesday* was released, hippies were well established and drugs were booming. Sandwiched in between the huge flop of *The Chase* and the sexually "decadent" *The Game Is Over, Any Wednesday* came and went without much notice, a modest success that became dated within a few years. America was choosing up sides, and the innocuous romantic couple, Jane Fonda and Dean Jones, in less than a decade became in real life a feminist-activist and a born-again Christian.

Jane was neither sexy nor very convincing in this movie. She spent most of her time in near-hysterics or crying a river over Robards and the trauma of turning thirty without a wedding band.

REVIEWS:

Rex Reed, *New York Daily News: Any Wednesday* is a good example of the movies taking everything that is crisp and human about the stage and turning it into everything that is loud and vulgar and boring about Hollywood. Simply everything is wrong with this loud-mouthed movie based very loosely on Muriel Resnick's warm and funny Broadway play. The story of a 30-year-old mistress who never grew up (played with strokes of cotton-candy brilliance and big feet by Sandy Dennis onstage) gets all but stomped on with cleated boots by Jane Fonda. She is about as funny as a manic-depressive having her first nervous breakdown. She screams, weeps, beats the furniture, picks at her cuticles, and when she has no lines she just pouts and fusses with her fright wig. Her kooky little-girl apartment with its closet full of balloons has been turned into something that looks like the storage room of a Third Avenue version of the Salvation Army. Her taste could be described as early fruitcake. Her keeper, who was once a charming man with a sense of humor onstage, is now a leering, lecherous magnate on the cover of *Time* magazine who yells and belches without a trace of "real person" quality in a performance which suggests that Jason Robards has tired blood.

Time: Any Wednesday is a kind of sexual string quartet arranged for four players, each assigned a key in the same flat. . . . Alert to the under-

Jane Fonda hurriedly greets her lover, Jason Robards.

Jason Robards finds a man (Dean Jones) in his younger girlfriend's apartment.

124

tones of Muriel Resnick's comedy, even a prude could relax and enjoy it, secure in the knowledge that every vibrant innuendo was just a homily in disguise. . . . *Wednesday*'s girl of the hour is Jane Fonda. Looking tempting and wholesome, she cries a lot but wears her teardrops like costume jewelry. Produced on cue, the drops are merely decorative, unrelated to any real passions or real truths. . . . The tone is too strident, the color too bright, the running around from rooftop to picturesque playgrounds too aimless. The corporate energy expended to produce each tiny bit of titillation raises questions not of taste but of waste. Sex ought to seem less work, more fun.

Richard F. Shepard, *New York Times: Any Wednesday,* which was a bright bauble of hit

Rosemary Murphy and Jane Fonda watch an argument between fellow cabmates Jason Robards and Dean Jones.

125

stagecraft when it came to Broadway, emerges not much the worse for wear. . . . Jane Fonda's eyes widen appropriately, she gets hysterical, she pouts and she goes through these exquisite changes of mood like a barometer in an area of rapidly changing pressures. It's called for in the action and she delivers it with enthusiasm. Jason Robards is something else as a corporate smoothie, a philanderer whose wickedly roving eye makes him lust even for his own wife. It's not much of a challenge and his performance is no more than adequate. Rosemary Murphy, as his wife, is as magnificently effervescent as she was when she created the role on Broadway. . . . To take *Any Wednesday* on its own terms, it is a pleasant enough, somewhat overdrawn film that will dispose of a few hours painlessly.

Fonda is torn between two lovers: Robards and Jones.

Fed up with her life, Fonda is stopped from doing something rash by husband-to-be Jones.

The Game Is Over

Royal-Marceau, 1966. Directed and produced by Roger Vadim. Screenplay by Jean Cau, Roger Vadim, and Bernard Frechtman, based on the novel La Curée *by Émile Zola.*
PRINCIPAL CAST: *Jane Fonda, Peter McEnergy, Michel Piccoli, Tina Marquand.*

THE TITLE OF THE movie version of Zola's *La Curée* was unaccountably changed to *The Game Is Over* for English-speaking audiences. It is the classic story of a woman who marries an older man of means but falls in love with his son, a handsome, sensual young man. The story is shifted to modernday Paris, and Vadim used the opportunity to explore the attitudes and morals of rich French people, even though his principal cast wasn't French.

Though Vadim wasn't faithful to Zola, French critics extolled *Game*'s virtues, as did most American critics. The film established Fonda's dramatic potential on the Continent and displayed her skills to better advantage than *The Chase, Walk on the Wild Side,* and others. *The*

Husband Michel Piccoli watches Jane Fonda flirt with an older man at a Paris party.

Young wife Jane Fonda is disenchanted with Michel Piccoli.

Game Is Over also displayed a lot of its leading lady, and in the United States, the publicity centered more on her exposed figure than on her acting prowess. She criticized several of her American critics and pointed out that she was often taken more seriously abroad.

For all the hard sell and good notices, *The Game Is Over* was not a hit domestically, though it was indeed a smash in Europe. Unfortunately, *Game* also produced some rear-view and topless photos of Jane, taken on the set without her knowledge. The photos found their way into *Playboy* and caused a furor, by far overshadowing the movie. Fonda was incensed at the pictures and sued *Playboy* for invasion of privacy, explaining that when she appeared nude on film, it was as a fictional character, but in a magazine, it was different. The lawsuit dragged on and on, and she failed to win it.

Stateside, *The Game Is Over* is all but forgotten, but in France it is considered a minor classic, one of Fonda's outstanding achievements.

REVIEWS:

Liz Smith, *Cosmopolitan:* Could movie director Roger Vadim do it? Could he do for his ac-tress-wife Jane Fonda what he did for sex goddess Brigitte Bardot and for Catherine Deneuve? The answer is yes, he can and he has. *The Game Is Over* is one of the most beautiful movies I've ever seen, photographed with a wealth of imagination and taste, as well as a fabulous attention to fascinating details of current Parisian life. . . . The movie is enthralling. Once you've seen the opulence of these interiors and exteriors (filmed in glorious color with sensual filters) in a mature but not sneaky look at nudity, sex and romance, you'll know how the rich live and love. The acting is first-rate. Vadim really knows how to pull it out of people. Jane has never been so appealing.

Kevin Thomas, *Los Angeles Times:* Roger Vadim's films are visual memoirs of his amours. He has made love with a camera to former wives Brigitte Bardot and Annette Stroyberg, who glowed on the screen in response. But he has never made it so well as with Jane Fonda, the current Mme. Vadim, who is not only as gorgeous as her predecessors but also a gifted actress. Consequently, *The Game Is Over* is his best film since *Les Liaisons Dangereuses* and the finest of Miss Fonda's career. Never has she looked so beautiful—photographed in ravishing color by Claude Renoir, no less—or has been given such a good part, that of a woman who falls in love with her stepson, who is about her own age. Having trusted in Vadim completely, she creates a comprehensive portrait of a woman in love—her joys and sorrows, hopes and fears.

Dale Monroe, *Hollywood Citizen-News:* Roger Vadim's sardonic and sensual *The Game Is Over* is one of the best films of its genre ever to come from France. Bold, adult fare, with scenes of passion at times unnecessarily prolonged, *Game* is nevertheless a film of uncompromising artistry and originality. . . . *Game* is Vadim's best picture to date and is unquestionably Miss Fonda's finest screen portrayal. The actress has of late demonstrated her agility as a light comedienne in Hollywood films. *The Game Is Over* is the first opportunity she has had in some time to display her intense dramatic ability with such a probing, in-depth characterization as that of Renée, the pampered and selfish young wife of a middle-aged businessman.

Judith Crist, *New York World Journal Tribune:* In this luscious Technicolor updating of Émile Zola's *La Curée,* Roger Vadim firmly establishes himself as Ross Hunter of the *nouvelle vague* and Jane Fonda as Miss Screen Nude of '67 while equally firmly setting the intellectual cause of cinema back some 40 years. Seldom has such lavish and lush scenery, decor, flesh and photography been used to encompass such vapidity and slush—and used with such beguiling slickness and style that the film goes right to the top of our list of Perfectly Marvelous Awful Movies to Eat Chocolates and Play Russ Columbo Records By.

Rex Reed, *New York Daily News:* Roger Vadim's concoction *The Game Is Over* is the updated, jet-age version of a classic Émile Zola tale about a man's revenge on his unfaithful child bride who has seduced his own son. In the hand of Vadim it turns into a combination Southern Gothic horror fable and half Cocteau's *Les Enfants Terribles.* Although much of it is borrowed from other directors, it has everything a decadent study in perversion should have to make it look like more than it really is: a house like Xanadu transferred to the heart of Paris, surrounded by thickets and complete with a steam bath, a Garden of Eden for Jane Fonda (Mrs. Vadim) to prance about naked in, a goldfish pond for Fonda to swim naked in, and the most vicious group of German police dogs since the early Sherlock Holmes movies. It also has a

Jane Fonda finds happiness in the car and the arms of Peter McEnery.

dark, brooding Heathcliff master-of-the-house who wears hunting jackets and leaves town a lot on mysterious business trips; a beautiful rapunzel of a bride, reduced through boredom to playing a game with her sexy stepson. They dress up in Genghis Khan costumes, smear each other with cold cream, drive sportscars into rivers, set their bedclothes on fire and put them out with champagne, break up the furniture, smash up the gilt-edge mirrors (there are lots of gilt-edge mirrors because it's a Vadim picture and he loves gilt) and even shoot at each other with rifles.

There are some of the most indescribably sensual love scenes since the walls melted in *Phaedra* (including one in which a hot sax purrs seducitively as Fonda dances behind a smoked glass with her face covered by white cream), and endless shots in which the actors hop around in the buff (I counted seven full-face bare-breast shots of Fonda, whose father must be purple-faced with embarrassment). Vadim handles her as though she were the Venus de Milo and even demonstrates, whenever possible, her American influence on *him*. Simple French idioms like "a table" turn up in the subtitles as "chow time" and at one point he has Fonda arriving at the breakfast table singing Comden and Green's "Good Morning" from *Singin' in the Rain*.

The best thing about the picture is Claude Renoir's lush camerawork, which is remarkable even in a picture of such simple dimensions. Vadim's films are always better photographed than directed, but this must surely be his most beautiful to look at. Everything is shot as though color had just been invented, and the shots of a factory at Lacq (borrowed though the idea is from Antonioni's *Red Desert)* turns the screen into great walls of sulphur in pastel yellow against white smoke rising into a purple sky. *The Game Is Over* is easy on the brain and easier on the eye, but all of that half-hearted upper-class sexual depravity is enough to make one long for the dear departed days of Walt Disney.

Fonda clashes with her husband, Piccoli.

Jane Fonda mirthfully returns home after a romantic incident in the lake.

Hurry Sundown

Paramount, 1967. Directed and produced by Otto Preminger. Screenplay by Thomas C. Ryan and Horton Foote, based on the novel by K. B. Gilden.
PRINCIPAL CAST: *Jane Fonda, Michael Caine, John Philip Law, Diahann Carroll, Faye Dunaway, Robert Hooks, Burgess Meredith, Jim Backus, Robert Reed, Beah Richards, Madeleine Sherwood, George Kennedy.*

THE CONVOLUTED PLOT of *Hurry Sundown* included several subplots and characters, predominant among them Michael Caine, Jane Fonda, and their on-screen son. Jane was a wealthy white woman reared by a devoted black mammy and sympathetic to the blacks' plight. Not so, such villainous types as Judge Burgess Meredith or the majority of whites in this movie. Another couple—white trash, as it were, but not bigoted—were John Philip Law and Faye Dunaway. The plot hinged on the whites' attempts to keep some blacks from gaining ownership of their own land, with the whites resorting to arson, dynamite, and near lynchings. In the end, con-

Jane Fonda plays southern belle Julie Ann Warren.

science-stricken Jane abandons Caine for an independent life with her son. Incredibly enough, by film's end, the blacks, who have been dynamited out of their land, aren't the least bit bitter or vengeful, even going so far as to help the white folks clean up and start anew.

Hurry Sundown had high hopes as a message film and a major Otto Preminger production with an all-star cast. There was something for everyone, from sex to violence, church hymns to a trial, as well as laughs, tears, and a death scene. Though cast in one of the few sympathetic roles, Fonda came off perhaps the worst. In one tawdry, much-remarked-about scene, she got on her knees between Michael Caine's legs while he sat languidly in an armchair, and suggestively played a saxophone with an insinuating look on her face. It was so tasteless that the scene is invariably cut for TV showings. In another episode, Fonda was moved to slap Diahann Carroll's face after the black woman entered a white women's restroom.

Preminger asked Fonda to head the cast of the movie version of the lengthy novel *Hurry Sundown* because he had seen her in *The Chase,* another southern story with social intent. The producer-director admired her southern accent, and she wanted to do something worthwhile, with more lasting impact than *The Chase.* She considered Preminger "enormously talented, dynamic, charming—one of the rare ones who can be a showman and an artist at the same time."

The story behind the making of *Hurry Sundown* turned out to be better than the one on the screen. First, permission to film in Georgia was denied, so Louisiana was chosen as an alternative. Unfortunately, word got out among the Baton Rouge locals that Hollywood intended to make a movie about "niggers gettin' the best of us white folk," and the hostility toward the cast and crew was, in Carroll's words, "so hostile you could cut it with a knife." Threats to the safety and lives of cast and crew came in by phone and by mail, their tires were slashed, and the Bellemont Motel, where they were lodged, had to be guarded by police around the clock.

The actual village chosen for filming hap-

Jane Fonda is married to scheming Michael Caine, father of her son.

Jane Fonda rebels against white prejudices and alienates local VIPs.

133

pened to be a center of Ku Klux Klan activity. The filming proceeded with ease, for there were almost no curious bystanders, and the locals kept far away from the aliens. Fonda, who had been minority-conscious since childhood, got to see bigotry at first hand, and the two months were an educational experience. "I kissed a little Negro boy on the street in front of the courthouse," she said, "and the sheriff asked us to finish the scene, get out of town, and never come back.

"We had this swimming pool at the motel and I'll never forget the first day one of the Negro actors jumped into it. There were reverberations all the way to New Orleans. People just stood and stared like they expected the water to turn black!"

It wasn't an easy time for Jane. Besides the depressing racism, she wasn't especially close to other cast members, and Vadim visited her infrequently. During the shooting, the *Playboy* photos came out, and a $9.5 million lawsuit was instigated on two continents. Shortly after *Hurry Sundown* wound up, she and Vadim were informed that their marriage wasn't legal in France because it had not been registered with a French Consul in the United States. And about the same time, Peter Fonda was arrested for possession of marijuana. Publicity about "Henry's impossible kids" became even splashier and more irksome.

For all the good intentions of Preminger and company, *Hurry Sundown* was another monumental fiasco, doing almost no business in the Deep South and very little elsewhere. More than *The Chase,* it alienated both blacks and whites, and several of the reviews (by white critics) took umbrage at what they saw as a put down of the South.

REVIEWS:

Wilfrid Sheed, *Esquire:* The movie South is a mess in any language. Apparently its audiences have shrunk to a point where the most cautious directors feel free to insult it at will. . . . Good King Box Office prefers to leave it independent for now, as a horrible example and target for outrage. . . . At this point we might ask the nurse for a fresh metaphor. What brought this one on is a bunch of movies about the South which are rougher in tone than the latest movies about Nazi Germany. There are few sectors so devoid of pull that Hollywood feels free to speak its piece about them, so the South serves a definite purpose, like Polish jokes. It provides a setting for a certain kind of bad movie and also a certain kind of good movie that cannot be made elsewhere.

Hurry Sundown is perhaps too gamy an example of the bad Southern movie; to criticize it would be like tripping a dwarf. . . .

The Indians have been cleared, even the ancient Romans have a lobby (commanded by

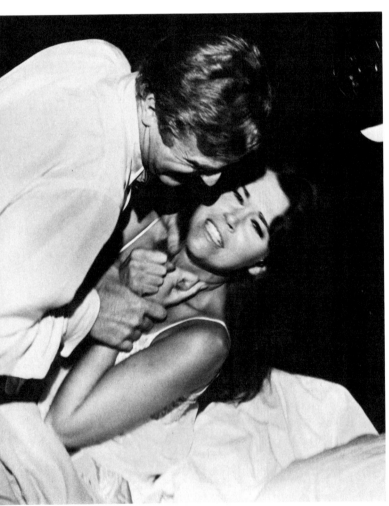

Caine and Fonda battle over the custody of their son.

thoughtful, troubled Frank Sinatra), but any damn fool can stomp on the South.

Judith Crist, *New York World Journal Tribune:* Gather roun' chillun, while dem banjos is strummin' out *Hurry Sundown* an' ole Marse Preminger gwine tell us all about de South. . . . The road to this disaster is . . . paved with good intentions (after all, being pro-civil rights is safe box office these days), as well as with tasteless sensationalism and plain and fancy foolishness. Otto Preminger has provided us not only with soap opera plotting that gives *Peyton Place* Dostoievskian stature but also with cartoon character and patronage of Negroes that are incredible in 1967.

The whole mélange would be offensive were it not simply ludicrous. . . . For villainy, there's Michael Caine, speaking a dialect that out-Remuses the old Uncle himself. Jane Fonda, Caine's wife, is a good kid, fond of her mammy and really pro-Negro and devoted to her retarded son. But she's hung up on Caine, a real love captive melting at his touch, getting all boozed up and stuff—you know how these decadent high-class Southern gals are. It's a new Jane, who doesn't even melt when Caine grabs her by the breast, and who sets out for the Meninger Clinic to get her son unretarded. . . . Those involved in this film deserve better than having their names repeated here. To say that *Hurry Sundown* is the worst film of the still young year is to belittle it. It stands with the worst films of any number of years. . . .

Shucks, you got to hear Jane Fonda say, "Mind if I crochet while we talk?" to get the flavor.

Andrew Sarris, *Village Voice:* Otto Preminger's *Hurry Sundown* has received much harsher reviews than it deserves. Charges of Uncle-Tomism are particularly unfair from critics who accepted and even applauded the Negro preacher and his psalm-singing daughter in *Nothing but a Man.* Still, Preminger has failed to integrate his personal dramas with the massive racial theme they are supposed to illuminate. . . .

Caine offers his willing wife another drink.

Preminger's sentimental affirmation in *Hurry Sundown* is still somewhat premature and grossly oversimplified, but I still feel this is a subject with which you are damned if you do and damned if you don't. . . . On the one hand, critics applaud *Ulysses* for its audacity in allowing Joyce's four-letter words to be recited on the soundtrack, and on the other hand, they denounce Preminger for a genuinely witty stroke of visual suggestiveness with Jane Fonda and a sex-ridden saxophone. Talk dirty but don't show dirty seems to be the McLuhanistic maxim of many of the reviewers. Yet the saxophone scene in *Hurry Sundown* is infinitely more daring and cinematic and, yes, truthful a breakthrough than the culture-mongering rehash of *Ulysses.*

Rex Reed, *New York Daily News:* Critic Wilfrid Sheed wrote recently in *Esquire* that "no movie is ever so bad that you can't find some virtue in it." He must not have seen *Hurry Sundown.* . . . Nobody has accused Otto [Preminger] of any particularly noticeable talents in recent years, but this time the Big O (as he is called by his co-workers) has pulled out all the stops in supreme bad taste. Except for *Laura,* Preminger's films have always been smelly examples of banality, badly directed and clumsily photographed, but shrewdly sold as items of controversy.

The white folks are all such mangy, degenerate critters that they are too ignorant to notice anything, what with Michael Caine (swallowing every syllable with a Cockney drawl so thick it is possible to decipher only about every fifth word) stealing everybody's land in between drivin' his little boy into a state of plumb mental ree-tardation by locking him in a hotel room, see, and driving his wife, Jane Fonda (just as scratchy and ill-at-ease in drama as she is in comedy roles) into a sexual frenzy so powerful she jes' falls between his knees and puts the butt of his saxophone right in her mouth with the slobber fallin' down her chin and all. . . . At the screening I attended the audience was hissing, booing and throwing popcorn boxes at the screen with such nasty vigor I almost missed the scene where the judge spit into the church communion cup. Unfortunately, they quietened down long enough for me to hear Jane Fonda gurgle, "I was 10 years old before I learned *damn* and *Yankee* were two different words."

The cast of Hurry Sundown, *including Michael Caine, Faye Dunaway, Robert Hooks, Jane Fonda, and producer-director Otto Preminger.*

Barefoot in the Park

Paramount, 1967. Directed by Gene Saks. Produced by Hal Wallis. Screenplay by Neil Simon, based on his play.
PRINCIPAL CAST: *Jane Fonda, Robert Redford, Mildred Natwick, Charles Boyer, Herb Edelman, Mabel Albertson, Fritz Feld.*

Barefoot in the Park was one of Neil Simon's earliest super successes on Broadway, starring Elizabeth Ashley and Robert Redford, both up-and-coming young stars. Its simplicity was part of its universal appeal, the story of two affluent newlyweds, he a stuffed shirt, she a free spirit trying to shake the cobwebs from his shoulders. Corie and Paul Bratter move into a fifth-floor Greenwich Village walkup in a building inhabited by so-called kooks. One of them is a Mr. Velasco, an aging hippie type who, among other eccentricities, walks through the Bratters' apartment to reach his own.

Corrie is delighted by the whole situation.

Robert Redford and Jane Fonda are loving newlyweds living in Manhattan.

Fonda and Redford inspect their walkup apartment.

Paul is appalled. To stir things up further, Corrie arranges a blind date for her stuffy mother with Mr. Velasco. The quartet dines at an Albanian restaurant, just one of the highlights of a most unusual night. The younger couple quarrels, and Corrie accuses Paul of being unable to let loose. However, Corrie's mother and Paul eventually develop some tolerance and spontaneousness, and the older woman spends the night at Velasco's apartment (platonically, of course).

Corrie finds Paul the next morning, drunk, carefree, and barefoot in the park.

The play was a sure thing, and so was the movie. Owing to the play's success, Elizabeth Ashley had a fairly good chance of securing the movie role but in the end producer Hal Wallis went with a name actress. Fonda reportedly helped ensure the casting of Redford in the film. Although the pair had worked together in *The Chase,* they became close friends while filming *Barefoot in the Park,* what with their numerous scenes together, the intimacy of those scenes, and their mutual liberal politics. Fonda later said, "Bob and I, we share the same causes."

(During their first two movies together, Fonda was the bigger box-office star, but in their third vehicle, *The Electric Horseman,* Redford got not only top billing, but a salary reportedly three times as large as Jane's one million dollars, plus a percentage of the profits. Ironically, in *Horseman* it was Fonda who played the career-minded urban square, with Redford as the free spirit— the opposite of their roles in *Barefoot.*)

Mildred Natwick was also retained from the play, as Corrie's mother, but Charles Boyer added glamour and star power (at least for older generations) in the role of Velasco. Redford, familiar with every nuance of the play, was able to "coach" Fonda in her role, which turned out to be her most celebrated comic performance to date.

Filming in New York went smoothly and quickly, fun for all the participants. The film was directed by newcomer Gene Saks, who thereafter directed several comedy and musical projects, such as the film version of *Mame,* which featured his wife, Beatrice Arthur. The charm-

138

ing Boyer, making fewer and fewer screen appearances, thoroughly relished this one. Of Fonda, married to a fellow Frenchman, he said, "She speaks very passable French, but she is American through and through.

"She has an eagerness to learn and do her role as well as she can. I don't always see that in established actresses. I understand her work for Vadim has been very sensual, but she seems very much at home in comedy, and there is a strong sexual undercurrent between her and Redford. They are almost too attractive a pair. . . . Jane is a friendly girl, though she does not laugh often and keeps a distance between herself and strangers. But she is compassionate, and she is concerned about more things than her hair or *maquillage*."

Barefoot in the Park, unlike Fonda's previous collaboration with Redford, received generally excellent reviews, which extolled the movie's entertainment value. It was one of her biggest hits, critically and financially. For the stereotypically handsome leading man, it was his first commercial success, the film that set him on the road to superstardom. Even today, audiences seem to prefer vehicles in which he is teamed with equally strong female partners, like Streisand and Fonda.

REVIEWS:

Kathleen Carroll, *New York Daily News: Barefoot in the Park* is the kind of picture that fills Radio City Music Hall with happy customers for weeks and weeks. The hilarious comedy . . . comes off better on the screen than on the stage. This is the best compliment that could be paid to the film—the original has been a hit since October 23, 1963. The improvement in the screen version can be attributed to the camera that moves the action out of a one-set presentation, showing incidents and sights around New York only referred to in the play. Each performance is a gem.

Time: Barefoot in the Park is one of the few plays to be reincarnated on-screen while playing on the Broadway stage. Happily, it loses little in

Jane Fonda and Robert Redford entertain mother-in-law Mildred Natwick.

transition. Essentially, author Neil Simon has taken a plot as bland as a potato, sliced it into thin bits—and made it as hard to resist as potato chips. . . . Jane's performance is the best of her career: a clever caricature of a sex kitten who can purr or scratch with equal intensity.

Fonda aids Natwick, on a double date with man of the world Charles Boyer.

Bosley Crowther, *New York Times:* If it's a romantic farce you delight in—old-fashioned romantic farce loaded with incongruities and snappy verbal gags—then you should find the movie version of *Barefoot in the Park* to your taste. . . . But if you are for a certain measure of intelligence and plausibility in what is presumed to be a takeout of what might happen to reckless newlyweds today, if you expect a wisp of logic in the make-up of comic characters which is, after all, what makes them funny, instead of sheer gagging it up, then beware.

Much of the early part of the picture, including a prologue honeymoon in the Plaza Hotel, is taken up with scenes of Miss Fonda osculating and running around in scanty attire. So voracious is her ardor, it's no wonder that Mr. Redford, who originated the role of the husband in the stage play and seemed reasonably relaxed in it, plays most of his scenes in a state of tenuous terror, as though fearful of being attacked—all of which makes one wonder how such a normal and nervous fellow could ever have got himself hooked up with this Kookie Kid.

Arthur Knight, *Saturday Review:* [Neil Simon] has an uncanny ear for the amusing turns of everyday conversation, which become funnier still when put into the mouths of people who take themselves very seriously. Simon's people, as represented in his own adaptation of his hit play, *Barefoot in the Park,* are essentially characters— which is to say that they are quite ordinary men and women operating under a strong compulsion to do ridiculous things, but who feel that their actions are the most natural and reasonable in the world. And because Simon makes them so attractive and appealing, we are more than willing to go along with them, enjoying every moment of their temporary discomfort, applauding enthusiastically their ultimate triumph. . . .

Jane Fonda, who hitherto seems to have had difficulty in determining which note to hit in her various roles, at last displays that she is in fact a charmingly fey, disturbingly sexy light comedienne, with an instinct for the timing and intonation of laugh lines that should keep her busy for many years to come.

Jane Fonda livens up a night out in Manhattan, with Charles Boyer, Mildred Natwick, and Robert Redford.

After a big argument the night before, Jane Fonda discovers hubby Robert Redford barefoot in the park.

Barbarella

Paramount, 1968. Directed by Roger Vadim. Produced by Dino de Laurentiis. Screenplay by Terry Southern, Brian Degas, Claude Brule, Jean-Claude Forest, Roger Vadim, Clement Wood, Tudor Gates, and Villario Bonaceil, from a book by Jean-Claude Forest.
PRINCIPAL CAST: Jane Fonda, John Philip Law, Anita Pallenberg, Milo O'Shea, David Hemmings, Marcel Marceau, Ugo Tognazzi, Claude Dauphin.

LONG BEFORE THE late 1970s, when there were plans to make movies of comic strips like *Superman, Popeye, Flash Gordon,* and *Sheena, Queen of the Jungle,* Roger Vadim decided to bring the European strip *Barbarella* to the screen as a supremely commercial vehicle for his wife. Indeed, after *Barbarella's* box-office thunder, unplain Jane was referred to as "the most fantasized-about woman in the world." In the years since Fonda's political consciousness was raised, *Barbarella* has often returned to haunt her. Yet she recently admitted, "I didn't hate making *Barbarella.* It was *fun* being her . . . for a while."

Unlike most American comic strips, *Barbarella* reeked with sex, and it was intergalactically spacey long before *Star Trek, Star Wars, Alien,* etc., made outer space a cinematic staple. Originally X rated, the movie was later censored to garner a more profitable rating, and today it is a favorite at movie-buff cinemas in campus communities, a vivid relic of the younger Jane Fonda of old, the unliberated but saucy sex symbol.

The most commented-upon segment of the French-Italian co-production was the beginning, the credit crawl behind which Fonda did a weightless strip tease while floating in what appeared to be a giant test tube. Another controversial scene, between Jane and Anita Pallenberg, had bisexual overtones, and then there was the invitingly fluffy nest of the handsome blind angel, played by John Philip Law in a loincloth. Jane had already sought Henry Fonda for a cameo role as the president of Earth. He asked, "Will I have to take my clothes off?" and de-

Jane Fonda as Barbarella, queen of the galaxy.

murred in favor of more conventional projects. He later said, "Jane has survived more bad movies than any actress should be able to in a lifetime."

It was her third movie for Vadim, and she was rather defensive about it. She felt her nudity was valid for several reasons, including the fact that the last of twenty-one sexy costumes had not arrived in time for shooting. "I don't think of it as an erotic film," she explained. "It's just funny and free and nice. You know, Vadim only has me completely nude behind the opening titles. He said, 'Everybody will be waiting for that, so why don't we get it over with right away and get on with the picture?' That's how he thinks about it all.

"If I have anything as an actress, I have variety. Why *not* go out on a limb and do something like *Barbarella?* It's fun, it's something new and different. Maybe making the picture wasn't as rewarding to me in the acting sense, day by day, but I like taking a chance like that. . . . I would never have done *Barbarella* with anyone else but Vadim. He convinced me that it was right for me, and I'm very glad he did." A decade later, she was inveighing against the Frenchman's "sexual exploitation of women."

Actually, she felt too much of her well-kept body was visible through the opening credits, and at her request Vadim edited the sequence, making it less explicit. But explicit or not, *Barbarella* was a smash success around the world, in those countries which didn't ban it. By today's standards it is tame and almost quaint, but as an imaginative fantasy, as a piece of nostalgia for times when toplessness was still shocking and actresses didn't take their politics seriously, *Barbarella* is still captivating.

REVIEWS:

John Simon, *New York Times: Barbarella* is a barely tolerable entertainment. Granted, almost any film that starts with Jane Fonda in the nude is doomed to going downhill from there. But at least Miss Fonda, even if approximately clothed, remains omnipresent, lending grace, suavity and a jocund toothsomeness to a foolish comic strip that emerges, in the movie version, a foolish comic strip. Terry Southern is the northernmost

Barbarella has an affair with the blind angel, played by John Philip Law.

Jane Fonda has survived an attack by a flock of killer hummingbirds.

Barbarella plots her strategy with David Hemmings.

In her fur-lined chamber, Barbarella receives orders to embark upon a new intergalactic mission.

among some eight, mostly French or Italian, perpetrators of this science-fiction grotesque, a kind of *Candy* in the sky with zircons.

There are some interesting props and actors (in that order) involved, but they are put to flabby and self-indulgent use. Typical of Southern and of Roger Vadim, the director and Miss Fonda's husband, is the submersion of some vaguely funny lines and situations in masses of spurious chic and gutless parlor sadism. By the latter I mean a flaccid, jaded appeal to our baser appetites, always liberally doused with essence of cop-out, resulting in an elucubrated, anemic pornography. The only episode approaching true wit is one in which the cosmos-trotting heroine is to be tortured to death inside a pleasure machine, an orgasm-organ; but that is a brazen plagiarism and vulgarization of the superb invention in Alfred Jarry's *Le Surmâle*. For this (or any other) film of his, Vadim deserves that Miss Fonda leave his bed and boredom, not to mention his cameras.

Charles Champlin, *Los Angeles Times:* You could subtitle the film *2002: A Space Idiocy.* Miss Fonda plays what you might call Flesh Gordon, and our first fetching view of her is as she does a strip tease floating in a state of weightlessness. We all get to appreciate the lack of gravity of the situation. (Her disrobing is technically ingenious and quite lovely, and many of the effects in the movie are equally ingenious, but never again quite so lovely.) As a film, *Barbarella* remains a thinking man's venture, although the thought required is minimal. In fact, the whole movie gives weightlessness a new definition. . . . It is impossible to evaluate performances in the traditional sense. Miss Fonda plays it straight, preserving the joke by taking things seriously though not earnestly. The real credit goes to Vadim and the artists who constructed this camp visit to outré space. It is a special taste, and not for your junior birdmen, but a foolish little something for the big birds.

Andrew Sarris, *Village Voice: Barbarella* is not nearly the disaster it had every intention of being. Somehow its comic strip conceits and Playboy-Bunny-in-Disneyland decor manage to sus-

144

tain themselves for 100 minutes without getting too heavy or too silly. Terry Southern is listed among the multiple writing credits and I suppose he can be credited with some of the literate tone in the gags, most of which sound better than they read. But the one indispensable ingredient in this confection is Jane Fonda, not only as the ideal Barbarella but also as perfect casting for Babs whenever someone gets around to filming Southern's *Flesh and Filigree.* From her opening space-suit strip tease through every single and double entendre in the script and gadgetry, our Jane manages to exude the kind of healthy girlscoutish non-campish sexuality that should be as accessible to our children as the morbidly repressed Peter Pansy entertainments now to be imposed on them via classification.

Rex Reed, *New York Daily News:* Glossy science fiction trash, which appears to be *2001: A Space Odyssey* seen through the eyes of Helen Gurley Brown and photographed by *Vogue,* and which never makes use of its opportunities, which is okay with me, since its opportunities are probably appreciated best by Harvard boys who sit around the *Crimson* office after school reading *Story of O* aloud to each other. I have learned through experience not to expect much from the art nouveau direction of Roger Vadim anymore (although I remember with fondness *Blood and Roses,* his particularly endearing confection about jet-set vampires and, unmistakably, his best film), but I find his manipulation of Jane Fonda increasingly more indigestible with each successive film. In this smoker room version of an intergalactic *Candy,* she is required to do nothing more than coordinate a certain toss of her mane with a certain toss of her mammary glands. Miss Fonda, I am happy to report, is in excellent physical shape for the assignment.

Pauline Kael, *The New Yorker:* What would Henry James have made of Jane Fonda, an actress so much like his heroines—an American heiress-of-the-ages abroad, and married to a superb example of the Jamesian villain, a sophisticated European . . . . Yet Roger Vadim's evil is reassuringly "wicked"—it's so obvious that he tries to shock only to please. And Jane Fonda

During her interstellar voyages, Barbarella encounters various menacing forms of life—some of them very strange.

Barbarella and her adversary Anita Pallenberg are rescued from danger by the blind angel.

having sex on the wilted feathers and rough, scroungy furs of *Barbarella* is more charming and fresh and bouncy than ever—the American girl triumphing by her innocence over a lewd comic strip world of the future. She's the only comedienne I can think of who is sexiest when she is funniest. (Shirley MacLaine is a sweet and sexy funny girl, but she has never quite combined her gifts as Jane Fonda does.)

Jane Fonda is accomplished at a distinctive kind of double-take: she registers comic disbelief that such naughty things can be happening to her, and then her disbelief changes into an even-more comic delight. Her American-good-girl innocence makes her a marvellously apt heroine for pornographic comedy. She has the skittish innocence of a teenage voluptuary; when she takes off her clothes, she is playfully and deliciously aware of the naughtiness of what she's doing, and that innocent's sense of naughtiness, of being a tarnished lady, keeps her from being just another naked actress. According to Vadim, in *Barbarella* she is supposed to be "a kind of sexual Alice in Wonderland of the future," but she's more like a saucy Dorothy in an Oz gone bad. . . .

In a dramatic turn of events, Jane Fonda battles Anita Pallenberg to rescue the blind angel.

Spirits of the Dead

American International, 1969. Directed by Federico Fellini, Louis Malle, and Roger Vadim. Produced by Les Films Marceau-Cocinor. Screenplay by Federico Fellini, Louis Malle, Roger Vadim, Bernardino Zapponi, and Daniel Boulanger, from stories by Edgar Allan Poe.
PRINCIPAL CAST: Brigitte Bardot, Alain Delon, Jane Fonda, Peter Fonda, Terence Stamp.

PORTMANTEAU FILMS, or suitcase films—divided into sections—rarely do well in the American market, and *Spirits of the Dead,* a misleading title for a triad of liberally handled tales by Poe, was no exception. (Its French title was *Histoires Extraordinaires.*) Jane and Peter Fonda were directed in the "Metzengerstein" sequence by, respectively, their husband and brother-in-law. Although they only played cousins, the strong incestuous overtones were perhaps intended to attract and thrill potential moviegoers.

Jane denied that the story was incestuous: "It was not our intention to 'titillate' this way, and in Europe, at least, no one took it like that. Not that I'm against incest, but our style is more direct. When the time comes for incest we will do it head on and leave the titillating for others. Give us credit, at least, for honesty."

Peter had earlier wanted to cast his sister in a movie of his own, titled *The Yin and the Yang,* in the role of Crass Commercialism, but nothing came of the project. The siblings played Frederique and Wilhelm in Vadim's portion of *Spirits of the Dead.* The plot was ambiguous, concerning a mysterious horse who may or may not have been the incarnation of Frederique's dead cousin and lover, Wilhelm. This segment also contained an orgy, a scene involving bisexual posturing, a handsome castle, and lush French countryside.

The shortish "Metzengerstein" at times seemed merely an excuse to show off peekaboo Renaissance-style costumes, as well as the famous Fonda curves (Jane's, that is). Critic Judith Crist opined that "the bare bones of Jane Fonda are getting to be a cinematic staple," and Molly

Jane Fonda as the sensuous, mysterious Frederique.

147

Haskell bemoaned the dearth of decent roles for American actresses like Fonda. Writing about chauvinistic directors like John Huston, Haskell noted, "Horses are another matter, and to them go the choice parts and the superior sensibilities. Were it possible for a woman to metapsychose into a horse, the way Jane Fonda did in Roger Vadim's 'Metzengerstein,' she would be assured a place of honor in Huston's films."

The only portion of *Spirits of the Dead* acceptable to most critics was the Fellini-directed sequence, set in modern Rome. So few Americans saw this film that most domestic moviegoers believe Jane and Peter have never worked together. One can assume their next joint effort will be more coherent and worthwhile.

REVIEWS:

Vincent Canby, *New York Times:* Vadim exhibits his wife, Jane Fonda, in various preposterous poses as a medieval woman who carries on a sort of love-hate relationship with a horse. This isn't as bad as it sounds, because the horse is really her dead lover who, when seen briefly, is none other than Peter Fonda. This, of course, adds another peculiar dimension to the film, which, like the absurd dialogue, is quite intentionally funny. The episode is beautifully photographed by Claude Renoir, and Jacques Fonteray designed Miss Fonda's clothes as if he were packaging a life-size Barbarella doll.

Enrico Zanghi, *Oggi: Les Histoires Extraordi-*

Jane and Peter Fonda, in their only co-starring film.

148

Jane Fonda as an expert archer and horsewoman, surrounded by her court.

naires is a series of unfinished stories having nothing to do with each other. Or even with themselves. The most remarkable thing in the movie is Bardot as a brunette. There is passion between her and Delon, but the passion between Peter and Jane Fonda is clumsy and embarrassing. . . . The Fellini contribution is the most powerful. The most confusing and expensive part is Vadim's. One wonders how much longer Jane Fonda will be popular in America, or elsewhere, if she makes more movies like this.

John Simon, *New York Times: Spirits of the Dead* is a trilogy of tales from Poe. The first episode, "Metzengerstein," was directed by Roger Vadim, making little further comment necessary. There may be worse filmmakers than Vadim, but no one can surpass him in spiritual rottenness. His is a megalomaniacal interior decorator's world inhabited by campy marionettes. His orgiasts have sawdust in their heads, veins and glands, and Vadim, for all his sexual shadowboxing, cannot even rise to that nadir of eroticism, dishonest titillation.

149

Jane Fonda roams the medieval French countryside in search of adventure.

Out riding with her court, Jane Fonda is about to discover her lover, played by Peter Fonda.

Here, at best one can get a laugh out of Jacques Fonteray's costumes, the ultimate in Folies-Bergères medievalism; we are treated to sheer medieval nightgowns, see-through medieval bodices, bared medieval midriffs and any number of interesting fashions to be burned at the stake for. The chief *frisson* is that Jane Fonda's love interest is played by her brother Peter, but since he cares more for his horse than for Jane and perishes before either passion can be consummated, no new frontiers are conquered. Particularly disheartening is the indifferent cinematography by the great Claude Renoir.

Bob Salmaggi, *New York Column.* Each director contributes an individual segment and, consequently, his own individual stamp. Vadim seems to have tailored his portion strictly for his wife, Jane Fonda. The time period seems to be that of the Renaissance, but Miss Fonda's array of clothes is way-out ultra-ultra *haute monde,* running to thigh-high boots, see-through panelings, chic fur ensembles, all giving extremely generous views of the Fonda anatomy. . . . It's a mood piece, nothing sensational but visually interesting with fleeting suggestions of perverted leanings running through the thing . . . and well, the feelings Miss Fonda has for her horse are a bit much. But as they say nowadays, whatever turns you on. The camera work, incidentally, is excellent. Good fluid shots of the bleak castle, the misty heath and the sea foaming under lead-colored skies.

Back at the château, the versatile Jane Fonda, as Frederique, indulges in sisterly love.

They Shoot Horses, Don't They?

Cinerama, 1969. Directed by Sydney Pollack. Produced by Irwin Winkler and Robert Chartoff. Screenplay by Robert E. Thompson, based on the novel by Horace McCoy.
PRINCIPAL CAST: *Jane Fonda, Michael Sarrazin, Susannah York, Gig Young, Red Buttons, Bonnie Bedelia, Bruce Dern, Al Lewis, Allyn Ann McLerie.*

GLORIA (JANE FONDA) is a young woman of the Depression. She is old for her years and doesn't feel life is worth much, having been betrayed and cheated several times in her young life. Fantasizing about movies, she sees herself as an actress and decides to head for Hollywood, having got the idea from a movie magazine while recuperating in the hospital after taking poison because of a man.

Gloria is perhaps the most memorable character ever written by Horace McCoy, who was a scenarist for more than seventy movies. His 1935 novel *They Shoot Horses, Don't They?* had a small readership, but over the years it became a cult novel in France, where luminaries like Malraux, Sartre, Gide, and De Beauvoir hailed it as an existential masterwork. After France brought it to America's attention in the sixties, it did well here in paperback.

The hero of *Horses* is Robert (Michael Sarrazin), a desperate Hollywood citizen unsuccessfully trying to become a director, never doubting that he'll eventually make it. Robert and Gloria meet, then decide to enter a dance marathon, one of the crazes of the thirties. The grueling dancing takes its toll on Gloria's already weakened, dark spirit, and she tells her boyfriend that she'd be better off dead, that her life is hopeless—all the while acting cruel and bitter, alienating those around her, and finally convincing Robert to shoot her and put her out of her misery: They shoot horses, don't they?

The story is narrated by Robert, with liberal use of flashbacks (such as the symbolic shooting of a white stallion) and flashforwards (like Robert's trial for shooting Gloria). It is a grim tale,

Jane Fonda in her first Oscar-nominated role, Gloria, the girl without hope.

commencing with Gloria's suicide attempt and ending with her demise at her boyfriend's hands, through her own influence. The marathon dance is used as a metaphor for the human spirit, and the fabric of *Horses* is enriched by other sharply etched characters, including the notable Rocky (Gig Young, who won a supporting-actor Oscar), an entrepreneur-MC who is hard bitten, tough, and devious, the opposite of Young's usual roles in Doris Day comedies and other light fare. Additional memorable parts were played by Susannah York, as a Harlow-like would-be actress just this side of ridiculous, and Bonnie Bedelia, as a pregnant Okie wife. Bruce Dern is Bedelia's ignorant, fanatical husband, and Red Buttons is an overaged marathon contestant who dies on the dance floor.

It is likely that Jane Fonda would have taken the lead in *They Shoot Horses Don't They?* even if she hadn't been paid the then-high sum of four hundred thousand dollars plus a percentage of the profits! She must have recognized it as the role of her career, just the thing to turn her into a bona-fide actress once and for all. She threw herself into the project body and soul, joking, "I look so scruffy in the part that I'll probably never get another." She even began staying overnight on the set, to stay in character, and Vadim later said, "She was working like a demon."

It was a difficult time for the superstar, who was also rethinking much of her life, including her ailing marriage. When a German journalist asked her, "How are you today?" at the start of an interview, Jane told her, "I'm thinking of getting a divorce." Her free time was devoted to her baby daughter, but she managed to read and reread Horace McCoy's novel.

"She was completely involved and totally professional," recalled director Sydney Pollack. "She carried a copy of the book around with her, and because she had strong opinions about it, she was slow to be persuaded if she disagreed with somebody else's interpretation of a point or a scene. That was so much more exciting than working with a puppet. She had a kind of re-

Jane Fonda decides to enter a dance marathon with Michael Sarrazin.

Fonda's relationship with Sarrazin is the only thing that buoys her above her suicidal tendencies.

Fonda's abrasiveness and pessimism take their toll on a marathon contestant.

mote quality. There was no socializing at the end of the day, no need to send her flowers or give her the 'Good morning, dear,' treatment. She wanted none of that."

Eventually Fonda moved into the set, dwelling in a trailer with her daughter, Vanessa, and a nurse. Insiders said she was determined to deliver Oscar-caliber work and prove herself, no matter what it took. As yet another Southern female, a Texan, she gave everything she had to the role, with little left over for Vadim, who remarked, "I do much more giving than Jane. In a way, in our relationship, she is the man and I am the woman."

Her efforts paid off beautifully, and though some critics received *Horses* with mixed emotions, they were unanimous in praise of Fonda's performance. She had progressed far enough to win her first Oscar nomination, and she received the prestigious New York Film Critics Circle

Award as Best Actress of 1969. But the part of Gloria also drained her, and she felt she needed time to think things out, as she headed into the seventies. She declared she had to place herself "into a position of extreme loneliness." That led to her milestone trip to India, which in turn led to her irrevocable politicization and antiwar activities. A divorce and the end of the sexy-girl-next-door image were right around the corner.

REVIEWS:

John Mahoney, *Hollywood Reporter:* Miss Fonda is the embittered Gloria who knows that life was rigged before she got there, longs for death and is yet incapable of executing the sentence she has cast. While all of her lines bespeak her longing for death, her weary and angry regard for life, so much of the film is conveyed through an unspoken subsurface, the unspoken responses that reveal the soul of the tormented creatures of the arena. And it is on this level that Miss Fonda reveals the longing, the vulnerability, the momentary hopes and the capacity for further injury which enrich the role and the film.

Pauline Kael, *The New Yorker:* A movie of Horace McCoy's 1935 "classic" Hollywood novel *They Shoot Horses, Don't They?* was long overdue. Like Nathaniel West's *The Day of the Locusts, They Shoot Horses, Don't They?* deals not with the movie business but with the people drawn to Los Angeles because that's where the movies come from. In the Depression years especially, it was a gathering place for the rootless and dispossessed, who hoped to find a new life in the movie sunshine.

Fortunately, Gloria, who is the raw nerve of the movie, is played by Jane Fonda, who has been a charming, witty nudie cutie in recent years and now gets a chance at an archetypal character. Sharp-tongued Gloria, the hard, defiantly masochistic girl who expects nothing and gets it, the girl who thinks the worst of everybody and makes everybody act it out, the girl who can't ask anybody for anything except death, is the strongest role an American actress has had on the screen this year. Jane Fonda goes all the way with it, as screen actresses rarely do once they become stars. She doesn't try to save some ladylike part of herself, the way even a good actress like Audrey Hepburn does, peeping at us from behind "vulgar" roles to assure us she's not really like that. Jane Fonda gives herself totally to the embodiment of this isolated, morbid girl who is determined to be on her own, who can't let go and trust anybody, who is so afraid of being gullible that she can't live. . . .

John Simon, *New York Times:* In the movie, Gloria is so dynamic, resourceful and clever that we cannot see her as the loser Rocky, the marathon's shady entrepreneur, recognizes in her. . . . I am not even persuaded that the strong-willed Gloria would need the bland Robert to act as her executioner. Here the fault lies partly in the movie-Gloria's greater attractiveness and less pronounced death-wish than her

Michael Sarrazin's grim determination supports Fonda.

Fonda's despondency and bitterness brings her into conflict with other marathon contestants.

Eventually, even Fonda's strength wears thin, and she is ready to be put out of her misery: "They shoot horses, don't they?"

fictional prototype, and partly in Michael Sarrazin's not being a good enough actor to convey how one may be swept into this deathly compact at the cost of one's own life. I think of an actor like Gerard Philipe in this part.

Pollack and Thompson have created two especially memorable characters: Gloria, the girl with the death-wish worn on her sleeve, and Rocky, the low-grade, hardened showman, are both absorbing and rich in surprises. At every turning point of the film they reveal something further of themselves—sometimes unexpectedly better or worse than we would have thought, sometimes thoroughly fulfilling our aroused expectations. And both are played very nearly to perfection.

As Gloria, that fine little actress, Jane Fonda, graduates into a fine big actress. . . . [She] here gives an antipodal performance: there is none of the glitter, kittenishness or jollity that have been her specialties in the past . . . and there is something about her very toughness that repeatedly moves us. . . .

But, but, but. There remains the . . . ultimate increditibility of Gloria's suicide—at least as presented on the screen. Sydney Pollack says that the last straw is supposed to be the accidental ripping of Gloria's last pair of stockings, and I concede that such an absurdly anticlimactic minor mishap will drive the exasperated person over the brink. But either because the incident is not etched sharply enough or because too much time . . . intervenes between it and the shooting, Gloria's death remains unconvincing.

I suppose this is partly due also to her not being made into enough of a loser in other episodes of the film, and to Jane Fonda's deep, vital attractiveness, which even the dark triumphs of make-up, costuming and performance cannot quite overshadow. Still, although *They Shoot Horses, Don't They?* does not, as a whole, reach the domain of art, many of its aspects and an aura that lingers on establish it as a true and eminent cinematic achievement.

Klute

Warner Bros., 1971. Directed and produced by Alan J. Pakula. Screenplay by Andy K. Lewis and Dave Lewis.
PRINCIPAL CAST: *Jane Fonda, Donald Sutherland, Charles Cioffi, Roy Scheider, Dorothy Tristan.*

JOHN KLUTE IS A smalltown policeman. Six months ago, a friend of his disappeared without a trace, and no one has officially been able to help Klute in the search. The missing man had allegedly written obscene letters to one Bree Daniel, a New York call girl. Klute sets out for the Big Apple to find Daniel and seek information from her. The two become grudging friends, learn to trust one another, and finally fall in love. Meanwhile, the search continues, and Bree goes about her business; she also visits a female psychiatrist to figure out her motivation for being a prostitute and to discover how she might possibly get out of the profession.

Klute concentrates on the unusual love story between Donald Sutherland and Jane Fonda, somewhat at the expense of the complicated, chilling plot. *Klute* is also a definitive portrait of a modern prostitute, as delineated by Fonda in what was widely acclaimed as her best performance yet. Though sexual, Bree was not sexy à la *Barbarella*, but a flesh-and-blood woman trapped by circumstance and smart enough to want to get out. The film's tone was neither pitying nor judgmental but at times had a documentary flavor, particularly in the sessions in which Bree explains to her shrink about her job and her reactions.

By film's end the killer has been traced, turning out to be a totally unsuspected hotshot, one of many men who wanted Bree Daniel but never knew her in the way the gentle John Klute did. The ending was upbeat but subdued by the inference that the former call girl may return to New York or find a new, solo way of life.

In typical Method style, Fonda prepared for *Klute* by speaking with high-class call girls in

Jane Fonda in her first Oscar-winning role, as Bree Daniel, call girl.

157

Manhattan, discussing their work and lifestyles. She didn't have to do very extensive research, however, for the role was painstakingly written beforehand.

The whole project was unorthodox, risky, and highly challenging. Director-producer Alan J. Pakula admitted, "It's a film I would not have done without Jane. I had met her a long time before, but I never really talked in any depth with her until a couple of weeks before I was sent the screenplay. . . .

"But I met Jane, and we talked for several hours about a lot of things—about women in our society, about sexuality in our society. It was just a wonderful, freewheeling discussion. I came out of it thinking, 'I'd love to work with that woman.' About two weeks later the *Klute* script was sent to me, and I called her immediately."

After she got the script Fonda was unsure about her feelings; one insider said she wasn't eager to get back to playing "easy women" after her excellent, image-breaking work in *Horses*. Pakula recalled, "She said, 'I don't know what I feel about it.' We talked for a half hour; she had an interviewer waiting and she had to get rid of me. She said, 'Look, do you really want to do it?' I said yes. She said, 'Okay, I'll do it.' Out of such little statements things get made."

By the time the movie started shooting, Pakula found "Jane had changed considerably. She had become firmly politicized, and she came to the set with this great passion—about everything, really—and I was concerned that her mind was not going to be on the film. She was very involved in so many causes. But she has this extraordinary kind of concentration. She can . . . make endless phone calls . . . and seem to be totally uninterested in the film. But when you say, 'We're ready for you, Jane,' she says, 'All right, give me a few minutes.' She just stands quietly for three minutes and concentrates, and then she's totally and completely in the film, and nothing else exists. And when the scene is right . . . she goes right back to the phone, and that other world is total. It's a gift good actors have; she has it to an extraordinary degree."

Klute was Fonda's first film since her trip to India, with its intensely affecting aftermath. For

Jane Fonda, as Bree Daniel, pounds the pavements of New York City, looking for potential customers.

the first time, her acting chores were mixed with political concerns, and it was on the set of *Klute* that she became known as the Mad Caller. She offered, "A year ago, for me to pick up the phone and call practically anyone except the people I was really intimate with was a trauma. I hated the telephone. I never answered the phone; Vadim always answered. . . . Now, I must make forty calls a day to people I don't even know . . . asking them all for favors, for money. I sometimes think, 'What am I doing? It's impossible that someone has changed this much!' "

Since the trip to India, Fonda and Vadim had grown apart, and Canadian actor-activist Donald Sutherland eventually took his place in her affections as well as co-starring with her in two subsequent films. Besides her acting, Jane was becoming more concerned with other aspects of moviemaking, and she didn't hesitate to offer an opinion or make a suggestion—or put her foot down, if need be. Pakula discussed *Klute*'s ending:

"You don't know what's going to happen to the call girl. Originally it ended with her and Klute laughing and loving their way down the street. . . . Jane said, 'There's no way I'll have anything to do with that,' and she was right. So it ends hopefully but enigmatically."

Fonda's first film of the seventies confirmed that *They Shoot Horses, Don't They?* was no fluke. The star was now a full-fledged actress, and her future projects would be chosen with much more care and thought than those in the sixties. Not all of them would be successful—due either to the material or to Fonda's new political assertiveness. For better or for worse, the Actress was here to stay.

Klute resulted in her second Oscar nomination and her first Academy Award.

REVIEWS:

Andrew Sarris, *Village Voice:* The murder mystery takes a backseat to one of the most affecting love stories of the '70s. Fonda and Sutherland peel away layers of suspicion to make emotional contact with each other, and Pakula seems more concerned with their relationship than with the rest of the plot.

Bree Daniel, who attends psychiatric sessions to find out what's "wrong" with her, here attends an actors' audition.

In her apartment after a trying day, Bree lights up a joint.

159

Molly Haskell, *Ms.:* Jane Fonda, in *Klute,* becomes a prostitute partly to exercise her acting ability but mostly to keep control of her life and her emotions, to avoid for as long as she can the trap of "falling in love." The ending of *Klute* is ambiguous: Fonda goes off with Sutherland but hints that she may occasionally return to New York, where she feels her real identity—fragile and negative as it is—to be.

Enrico Zanghi, *Oggi:* Jane Fonda gives an Oscar-quality performance in *Klute,* the scariest movie of the year. It is a thriller, a love story and a portrait of one woman: a prostitute who is intelligent, ambitious and virtually hopeless, but afraid to admit it to herself. Jane Fonda dominates the rest of the cast, and though she gives the best American portrait of a prostitute ever— infinitely more real than, for example, Shirley MacLaine's *Irma la Douce*—there is no excess of vulgarity, no sensationalism and no nudity, though there is suggestiveness, humor and a suc-

Suspicious Bree Daniel eventually comes to rely on, then falls in love with, Detective Klute, played by Donald Sutherland.

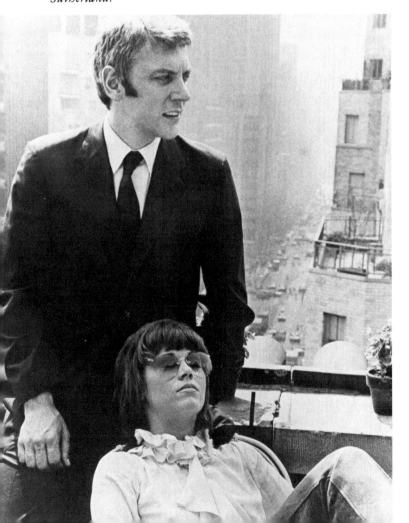

cessful effort by the producer-director to involve the audience with Bree and her story.

Roger Greenspun, *New York Times:* Alan Pakula's *Klute* . . . ought to be called *Bree* (or maybe *Miss Daniel*) because it is really about her and her problems—one of which happens to be a psychopathic killer. Bree Daniel (Jane Fonda) likes her job and she's good at it, but she's trying, without luck, to act on the stage. "Why do I still want to trick?" she asks her analyst. Her analyst, a most helpful woman, replies, "What is the difference? You're *successful* as a call-girl; you're not successful as an actress." Which is not strictly true, for Bree, who is a kind of Method call-girl, really does act when she tricks, and never more ambitiously than for a favorite customer, a 70-year-old garment cutter ("I'm all he's got") to whom she recalls the old-world glamour he has never known:

"Cannes was rather amusing. . . . We played baccarat and chemin de fer. . . . There was an intriguing older man. Nobody could tell me whether he was an exiled prince or a mercenary." And so on—all the while delicately stripping.

At one point in her way through the nightmare of her life Bree takes drugs. Klute (Donald Sutherland), who by this time has grown pretty attached to his only clue, patiently sees her through her withdrawal until she is cured. . . . The acting in *Klute* seems semi-improvisatory, and in this Jane Fonda, who is good at confessing, is generally successful. Everybody else merely talks a lot, except for Sutherland, who scarcely talks at all. A normally inventive actor, he is here given precisely the latitude to evoke a romantic figure with all the mysterious intensity of a youthful Calvin Coolidge.

Pauline Kael, *The New Yorker:* Jane Fonda's motor runs a little fast. As an actress, she has a special kind of smartness that takes the form of speed; she's always a little ahead of everybody, and this quicker beat—this quicker responsiveness—makes her more exciting to watch. This quality works to great advantage in her full-scale, definitive portrait of a call-girl in *Klute.* It's a good, big role for her, and she disappears into

Bree, the call-girl, so totally that her performance is very pure—unadorned by "acting." As with her defiantly self-destructive Gloria in *They Shoot Horses, Don't They?*, she never stands outside Bree, she gives herself over to the role, and yet she isn't *lost* in it—she's fully in control, and her means are extraordinarily economical. She has somehow got to a plane of acting at which even the closest close-up never reveals a false thought and, seen on the movie streets a block away, she's Bree, not Jane Fonda, walking toward us.

Bree's knowledge that as a prostitute she has nowhere to go but down and her mixed-up efforts to escape, make her one of the strongest feminine characters to reach the screen. It's hard to remember that this is the same actress who was the wide-eyed, bare-bottomed *Barbarella* and the anxious blonde bride of *Period of Adjustment* and the brittle, skittish girl in the broad-brimmed hat of *The Chapman Report*. I wish Jane Fonda could divide herself in two, so we could have new movies with that naughty-innocent comedienne as well as with this brilliant, no-nonsense dramatic actress. Her Gloria invited comparison with Bette Davis in her great days, but the character of Gloria lacked softer tones, shading, variety. Her Bree transcends the comparison; there isn't another young dramatic actress in American films who can touch her.

Bree acts as bait to help track down a vicious murderer, in a pursuit that becomes a nightmare for her.

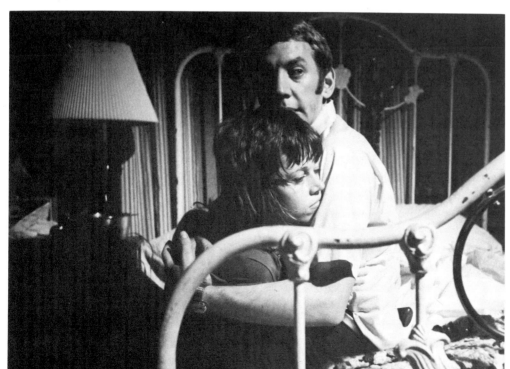

After a close call with death, Daniel finds refuge—but not necessarily her future—in the arms of Klute.

F.T.A.

American International, 1972. Directed by Francine Parker. Produced by Francine Parker, Jane Fonda, and Donald Sutherland. Written by Robin Menken, Michael Alaimo, Rita Martinson, Holly Near, Len Chandler, Pamela Donegan, Jane Fonda, Donald Sutherland, and Dalton Trumbo.
CAST: *Jane Fonda, Donald Sutherland, Len Chandler, Pamela Donegan, Michael Alaimo, Rita Martinson, Holly Near, Paul Mooney, Yale Zimmerman.*

As MOST AMERICANS and all army veterans know, F.T.A. stands for F—— The Army. However, to avoid offending puritan sensibilities, and to provide a new political interpretation of the abbreviation, the movie title was translated as *Free the Army*. During the Vietnam conflict, Fonda and

Antiwar activists Donald Sutherland and Jane Fonda star in the documentary of their touring stage show, F.T.A

other antiwar activists wanted to offer an alternative to the pro-war shows offered by Bob Hope and others. They called their troupe and their show F.T.A. (which they said could also be translated Free Theatre Associates), and their purpose was to instill the antiwar side of the issue in the soldiers' minds while providing them with much-needed entertainment.

However, the United States army would not allow F.T.A. to perform on its mainland bases, so the show traveled from army town to army town, settling into local GI coffeehouses and high school auditoriums. The skits and musical numbers were put together by a large number of individuals; as Jane began to take an active hand in putting together the film version of the show, there were reported rivalries and tensions within the troupe, and certain members accused others of caring more for their own careers and advancement than the politics they espoused.

The growing feminism Fonda displayed was another source of factionalism, especially among the men. In the end, she chose Francine Parker to direct and serve as co-producer. The political actress announced, "We're not going to do that kind of chauvinist show with topless dancers and a lot of breasts," referring to established GI entertainment. "If that's the only kind of entertainment soldiers can get, that's what they'll watch. But that's also why American men and soldiers feel women are to be used as sex objects. The violence against Vietnamese women is terrible, and those shows contribute to it."

Jane also became involved with Hollywood's Entertainment Industry for Peace and Justice, a group of celebrities trying to mobilize public opinion against the war. Membership included Barbra Streisand, Burt Lancaster, Sally Kellerman, Brenda Vaccaro, and Tuesday Weld, as well as many nonperformers in the movies and TV. Through the EIPJ Fonda met unknown women filmmakers like Francine Parker. A male friend of Jane averred, somewhat enviously, "They began convincing her that the GI show and everything else she appeared in ought to present women in a better light. They let it be known that they . . . could easily write and direct this pro-woman material."

The emphasis, however, was not so much feminist as antiwar, and the show F.T.A. received a mixed response from soldiers and civilians. Official opposition was tremendous, and publicity was mostly negative. When the movie version finally found a distributor in American International Pictures, the film hardly lasted more than a few days anywhere in this country. In Los Angeles it was "pulled" overnight, without explanation. The show received more publicity than the movie, which went unreviewed by most critics and is one of Jane Fonda's least-known cinematic efforts, not to mention one of the most unusual. Today it would no doubt be far less controversial than when it came out, but it is one Fonda offering that will probably never be seen on television.

REVIEWS:

London Movie Express: F.T.A. is an unlikely candidate for success and should be of particular interest only to fervent fans of Jane Fonda and confirmed "doves" concerned with the ongoing war in Southeast Asia.

Enrico Zanghi, *Oggi:* A very controversial documentary is *F.T.A.,* fueled by two women: activist-actress Jane Fonda and director/co-producer Francine Parker. In the United States, of whose government policy *F.T.A.* is outspokenly critical, it was banned in most places or unofficially boycotted. *F.T.A.* marks the low-point of Fonda's career in terms of her popularity among the American masses. . . . Her motivation is genuine and this documentary raises several valid points. It is probably not typical of all American soldiers and, therefore, is as much of a propaganda message as the pro-war propaganda messages which it denounces.

Roger Greenspun, *New York Times:* By now most people must know something about the political vaudeville troupe formed by Jane Fonda, Donald Sutherland and others to offer soldiers an alternative entertainment to, say, Bob Hope or whatever shows are provided by the U.S.O. The troupe called itself F.T.A., which stands for Free Theatre Associates or for

Jane Fonda, Donald Sutherland, and other F.T.A. *cast members, in one of the twenty-one episodes highlighted in the film.*

other things such as Free The Army. Last year, against considerable official opposition, it toured United States military bases in the Pacific. Francine Parker's *F.T.A.* is a documentary about aspects of that tour.

The film divides its attention pretty evenly between the performers and their audience, and a lot of time is given to interviews with dissident or disillusioned servicemen. . . . So much time is given to the audience, whose insights, though real, are neither original nor profound, that the actual performance comes across in scattered bits and pieces.

Occasionally the F.T.A. troupe becomes involved with the local population, so that we may hear the Just Grievances Against American Imperialism of the people of Okinawa or Japan or wherever Miss Fonda and her colleagues happen to be listening. I found most of this a predictable bore, but it did allow for the film's only really striking sequence: an anti-American guerrilla theatre pageant in the Philippines that momentarily turns revolutionary passion into a romantic gesture of extraordinary beauty.

Otherwise there are a few good things . . . some hints at lively routines, an occasional glimpse of deep happiness in eyes of Holly Near and Miss Fonda. But the spirit of *F.T.A.* must lie elsewhere, in other times and special places. For all its agility and pressing close-ups, the film doesn't capture that spirit.

Steelyard Blues

Warner Bros., 1972. Directed by Alan Myerson. Produced by Tony Bill and Michael and Julia Phillips. Screenplay by David S. Ward.
PRINCIPAL CAST: *Jane Fonda, Donald Sutherland, Peter Boyle, Howard Hesseman.*

IN *Steelyard Blues* Jane Fonda reprised her hooker character, in an Afro wig. Donald Sutherland was along for the ride again, joined by Peter Boyle's frequent Brando imitations. The movie, made in San Jose, was an amateurish production of vague liberal intent and nonsensical plot. The story follows a bunch of misfits trying to fix an old plane and fly off into the wild blue yonder. There was no sex in the film, in keeping with the new image Fonda was acquiring, but there were unfortunately needless vulgarity and low production values.

Jane was finding it harder to get work in the United States. Her next three films would all be made overseas and would fail miserably at the box office. This one failed too—it came and

Jane Fonda plays Iris, a part-time hooker.

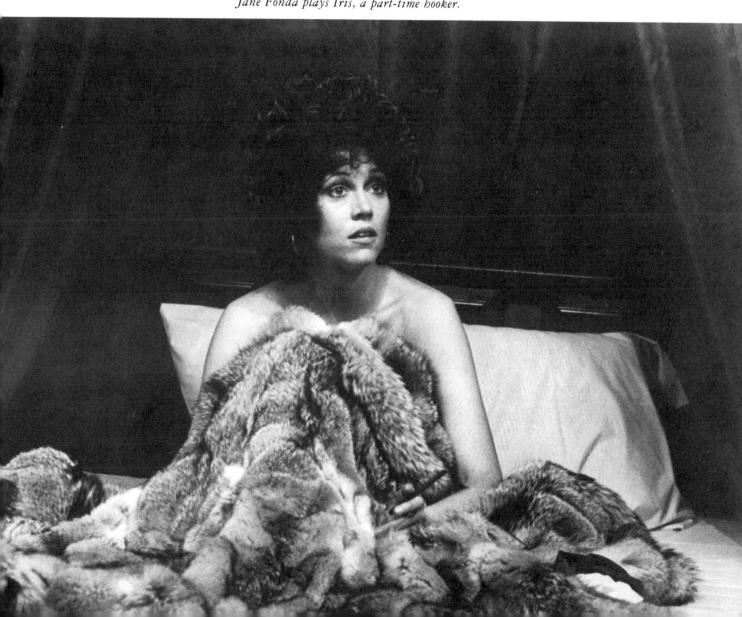

Jane Fonda strips a very important customer, Howard Hesseman.

Fonda collects payment from Hesseman, the district attorney.

went, and hardly anyone noticed. Oscar or no Oscar.

REVIEWS:

Motion Picture: Jane Fonda, who has played happily amoral kooks in the past, now seems obsessed with hookers as some kind of symbol of oppressed womankind, and the role is getting tiresome. After her significant portrayal in *Klute,* why repeat herself in a film that isn't even worth the watching? *Steelyard Blues* is almost as big a bomb as her recent *F.T.A.,* if that is possible.

London Movie Express: For Fonda fans, there is *Steelyard Blues,* which again pairs her with Canadian Donald Sutherland, who is wasted in his role as prince consort to the queen of American politics. There are some amusing moments as Peter Boyle tries on a Brando persona, but there's no sustaining interest here, and Fonda-watchers will be disappointed by her relative modesty and conservative attire.... This one didn't make it in the States, and probably won't fare much better here. Catch it while you can, if you must.

Pauline Kael, *The New Yorker: Steelyard Blues* might have provided material for a couple of "The Monkees" shows of some seasons back. It's about a band of thieves and hookers—meant to be adorably nutty—who, persecuted by the squares of this world, repair a plane by skill and theft, and plan to fly off to a better one. . . . With Alan Myerson's amateurish, erratic direction, the film never gets a rhythm going and doesn't draw us in. . . .

Jane Fonda plays a happy hooker, but she's just doing a long walk-through. She has charm—even without a character to play—but her and Sutherland's roguish complacency at being hip outlaws in a straight society isn't the charming nonsense they mean it to be. Their little digs and grimaces about the meanness of the straights are almost a parody of their offscreen characters, and it's embarrassing to watch them, because they've turned blithe exuberance into cant.

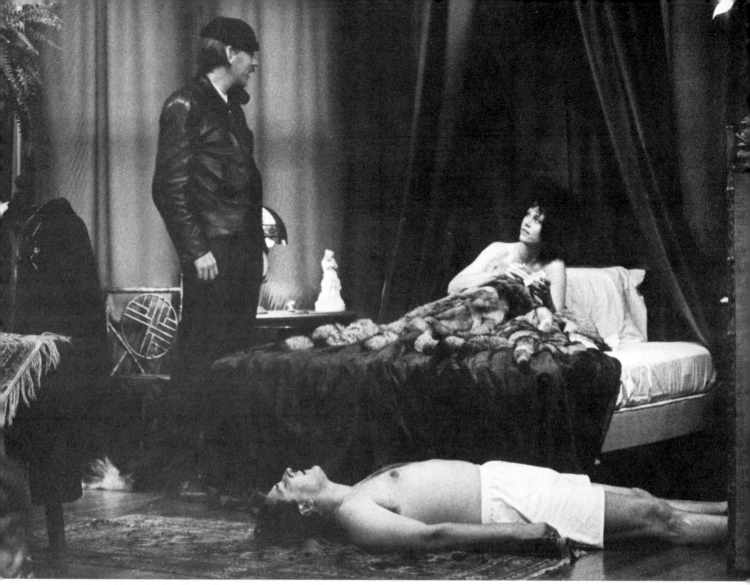

Donald Sutherland, as the D.A.'s unmaterialistic brother, discovers Jane and an overwhelmed visitor.

Vincent Canby, *New York Times: Steelyard Blues* is an appealing movie if only because all of the people connected with it seem so utterly convinced that they are making a Third World film disguised in the shape of an eccentric caper comedy. I like its earnestness, its brow furrowed with mission. It reminds me of the little boy who covered himself with vanishing cream and then walked through a dinner party in the fond belief he was invisible.

Sutherland, playing a sad-faced, gentle demolition-derby driver, gives the impression of someone who's too thin because his passion will not let him rest. He hasn't time for proper meals while he works on plans to wreck every car man-

ufactured in America between 1940 and 1960. His impossible dream: a giant demolition derby involving not just passenger cars, but dump trucks, school buses, pick-up trucks, delivery vans, trailers, campers and, at the finale, mobile homes.

Iris (Jane Fonda) is a $100-a-night hooker who does not know she's being humiliated until she's beaten up by the police at the direction of the district attorney (Howard Hesseman). He is not only an occasional customer but also Veldini's (Sutherland's) brother.

Eagle (Peter Boyle) hasn't any passion of his own. Eagle is a schizoid, out-of-work circus man ("There's not much call for human flies these

167

days'') who hasn't a thought one way or the other about the yoke of the automobile economy.... In *Steelyard Blues* liberation is represented by a plan to raid a navy yard to steal an electrical circuit that, in turn, will allow the innocents to fly off to a better world in a refurbished PBY of World War II vintage.

It may be because Miss Fonda's and Suther-land's soberly humanitarian left-wing political views are so well known that they lend a heaviness to *Steelyard Blues* that it would not have if we were not so aware. I doubt it, however. They are two performers I admire very much, but this film, which may be up to their politics, is not up to their talents. Their presence gives it more importance than the material warrants.

Fonda and Sutherland repair an old airplane, which they hope will take them to a better world.

Donald Sutherland, Jane Fonda, Peter Boyle, and friends realize their dream of reclaiming and repairing a plane, which offers them a new life.

Tout Va Bien (*Everything's Okay*)

New Yorker Films, 1973. Directed by Jean-Luc Godard and Jean-Pierre Gorin. Produced by Jean-Pierre Rassam. Screenplay by Jean-Pierre Gorin and Jean-Luc Godard.
PRINCIPAL CAST: *Yves Montand, Jane Fonda, Vittorio Caprioli, Jean Pignol, Pierre Ondry, Elisabeth Chauvin.*

JEAN-LUC GODARD was one of the most prominent French filmmakers of the *nouvelle vague.* His outstanding work was *Breathless*, with Jean Seberg. Over the years, the director grew more fiercely political, making Maoist statements in *La Chinoise* and examining Communism in *The Assassination of Trotsky* (with Richard Burton as the exiled politician), then undertaking the pedagogic *Tout Va Bien* ("Everything's All Right"). This much-anticipated—in France, anyway—film had as its central characters the nameless He and She, played by Marxist actor Yves Montand (married to fellow Marxist Simone Signoret) and Jane Fonda.

Jane Fonda and Yves Montand, as She and He, in the French political film Tout Va Bien (*"Everything's Okay"*).

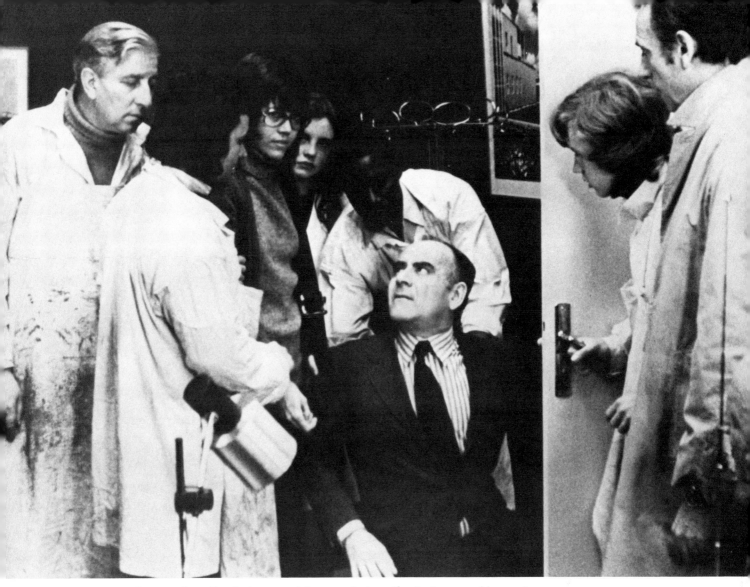

Reporter Jane Fonda is trapped in a worker's strike during one of her assignments.

Montand's He is a maker of film commercials, and Fonda's She is a dedicated journalist. The couple resides in Paris, and one day they visit a sausage factory, which is then taken over by political radicals. Fonda and Montand, as well as the audience, are lectured on the nuances of leftist politics, and by film's end, husband and wife have evolved to a state of extreme politicization. Ironically, their political awareness—including sensitivity to traditional gender roles—may threaten their marriage. Or it may not. The ending is the only indefinite part of this strange, nonentertainment movie.

Godard, along with his young collaborator Jean-Pierre Gorin, who received equal credit, had planned to make this film since the May 1968 student riots, which rocked Paris to its very foundations and radicalized thousands of students and workers. Fonda seemed a natural to play the role of the American journalist married to a Frenchman, and Godard had long preferred to work with WASP actresses. Besides, Fonda was still a big celebrity in France, despite her lengthy absence and her involvement with American life and politics.

While in Paris to shoot the film, Jane and daughter Vanessa stayed with five other women in a kind of feminist commune. At first, the actress was favorably impressed by Godard. She remarked, "Godard is the only person I've ever met who's truly revolutionary." Soon after, her admiration declined when she found that his

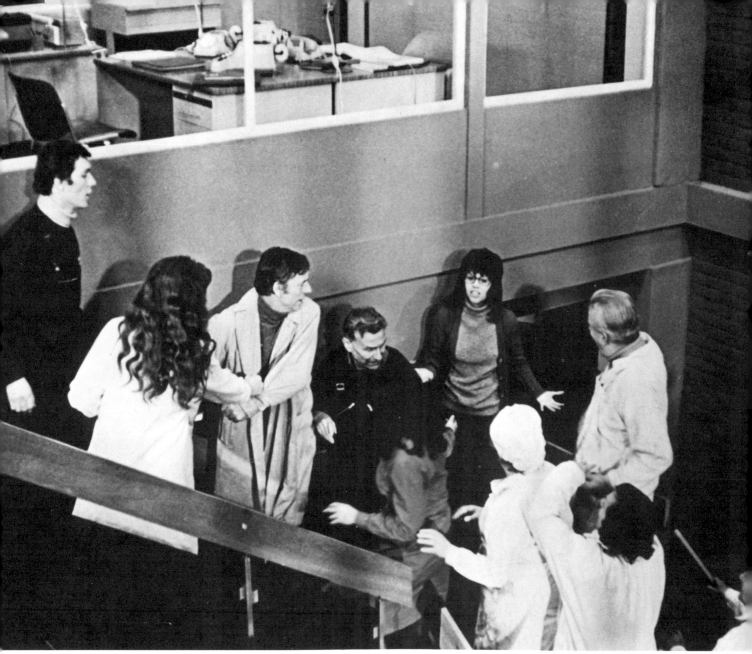

Montand and Fonda become radicalized and involved in a worker's strike in Paris.

methods of dealing with people weren't gentle or considerate. She declared she would rather work with someone whose political views differed from hers but who treated people better. "A true revolutionary," she explained, "has to care about people."

Tout Va Bien was given an almost nonexistent American release and made practically no money in this country, faring moderately better in France. For the most part, movie audiences weren't ready—and still aren't—for nonentertainment, and the leftist sentiments of *Tout Va Bien* and the people connected with it weren't a point of attraction for American audiences.

Fonda has since said she will never again fall into the trap of making movies that hit the audience over the head with a message. Entertainment, preferably with a soft-pedaled moral, is her cinematic aim, along with remaining true to her convictions as a feminist activist and a fine actress.

172

REVIEWS:

Vincent Canby, *New York Times: Tout Va Bien* stars Jane Fonda and Yves Montand, who are—in spite of their loudly proclaimed leftist (but hardly radical) political views—symbols of the bourgeois film industry on which Godard turned his back five years ago.

It is Godard's first revolutionary film for the bourgeoisie and, unless audiences are more indulgent than I credit them to be, it may well be his last. Although I find Jane Fonda most appealing (and very funny) as a solemn American political correspondent who becomes radicalized after being trapped overnight in a strike in a Paris sausage factory, I suspect that most people who go to movies would prefer to see her as the unhappy hooker for which she won her Academy Award.

After the strike, Fonda reasserts herself in front of husband Montand.

In two sequences, one shot at a TV studio and another at a Paris construction site, Montand, talking directly to the camera, describes the weariness with which he came to direct his fiction films and how he finally preferred to make commercials, which allow him to participate in the system without hypocrisy.

Miss Fonda has some equally fine moments near the end when, after She and He have been freed from the sausage factory, they sit having breakfast in their flat, the liberated She now furious with He who, though politically aware, remains impossibly chauvinistic where she's concerned. When we last see He and She, each is, says the narrator, rethinking himself in historic terms.

Samedi et Dimanche magazine: *Tout Va Bien* is a tedious, pretentious, boring and unconvincing political self-indulgence for those before and behind the camera. This kind of thing belongs in the classroom or on television during elections, not in the cinema. . . . No one in their right mind would pay money to be preached at so shamelessly.

Molly Haskell, *Ms:* Godard's feelings for women are remarkably similar to his feelings toward America—extreme love-hatred. His feelings toward America, symbolized in the recurrent images both sensual and repellent, of automobiles, are so personal they might easily be called "misogyny." His actresses are American or americanized. . . . The films in which Godard identifies with women's problems of a sociological nature are his least effective.

In his political films, Godard's self-hatred and, with it, his misogyny, increase. . . . His ambivalence toward America reaches a peak in his two most recent films, *Tout Va Bien* and *Letter to Jane*. In the latter, a "structuralist" essay made expressly for the New York Film Festival, he alternately chides and analyzes Jane Fonda for allowing herself to be used for imperialist-media purposes on her trip to North Vietnam; in *Tout Va Bien,* he betrays the ambivalence by which he associates America with "stars" by using Jane Fonda in the lead but by constantly shunting her off to the side so that the "proletarians"—his musical-comedy factory workers—can express themselves.

Roger Greenspun, *New York Times:* Jane Fonda plays She, an American correspondent in Paris, and Montand plays He, her French husband who used to write scripts for New Wave movies and now makes television commercials. One day She, on assignment, and He, along for kicks, are trapped in a workers' takeover of a sausage factory. The factory . . . contains a boss, straw bosses and women oppressed both by the bosses and the assemblyline men.

Everybody explains his position, and the boss is made a fool of, and by the time they leave the factory He and She have been radicalized to the point that they begin to see their lives not as isolated activities but as a unified whole—a whole that must be understood politically.

The factory is one great image of our society and later in the film there is another, a supermarket so enormous it might as well be another factory. Godard photographs the supermarket by tracking his camera back and forth in a straight line in front of the checkout counters, while goods are bought, a French Communist Party author hawks a book, young activists break in and a minor riot ensues.

Both Montand and Miss Fonda (speaking her own French) are expressive and energetic actors, and they provide *Tout Va Bien* with a measure of articulate brightness that is its pleasantest quality as a movie. . . .

A Doll's House

1973, shown on ABC-TV by Tomorrow Entertainment. Directed and produced by Joseph Losey.
Screenplay by David Mercer, based on the play by Henrik Ibsen.
PRINCIPAL CAST: Jane Fonda, David Warner, Trevor Howard, Delphine Seyrig, Edward Fox.

JANE FONDA SEEMED the ideal actress to essay the familiar role of Nora, the woman in the real-life doll's house who has her consciousness raised and leaves behind her husband and children in an attempt to find her own identity. Ibsen's classic is perhaps the most often-performed play from the nineteenth century; yet it hasn't often been translated into film. The 1970s, a decade of women's liberation, found *A Doll's House* more popular and relevant than ever, and at the same time that this production was being filmed in Roeros, Norway, a rival film, starring Claire Bloom as Nora, was being shot. Although Fonda was much the bigger star, it was the Bloom vehicle that won national release. The Fonda vehicle was never released

Jane Fonda stars as Nora, the unliberated wife, in Ibsen's A Doll's House.

Restricted to life in her Norwegian "doll's house," Fonda finds herself bored.

Stateside, owing to the poor box office of her last few films and the controversy encircling her name, but was acquired by Tomorrow Entertainment and shown on ABC-TV as a "world premiere" movie that garnered dismal ratings. On the other hand, the Bloom version bombed in the cinemas.

Joseph Losey, the man behind this version, is an American director who had to leave the United States in the fifties to escape political blacklisting. Ensconced in England, he became highly esteemed for directing critical and popular hits like *The Go-Between*. It would have seemed that Losey and Fonda, both highly political individuals, would get along smoothly, but it didn't turn out that way. For one thing, Jane became allied with French co-star Delphine Seyrig, an ardent feminist, and reportedly asked for aspects of the film to be made more pro-feminist. The Fonda-Seyrig faction supposedly alienated several male cast and crew members, and Jane was also heavily involved at the time with other causes.

Additionally, she became increasingly inseparable from Tom Hayden, and toward the end of

shooting, she announced her engagement to him. Insiders declared that the couple seemed unaffectionate with each other and were obsessed with politics. Losey recalled, "She was spending most of her time working on her political speeches instead of learning her lines, and making innumerable phone calls about her political activities."

Director and star came to an agreement, however, and the finished product contained a stunning performance by the actress. Unfortunately, Fonda went largely unpraised, thanks to the restricted release of *A Doll's House* and the widespread prejudice against her, which didn't really abate until her "comeback" in *Fun with Dick and Jane* and her reabsorption into the Hollywood mainstream.

Soon after shooting ended, Fonda participated in a demonstration against saturation bombing of North Vietnam by the Nixon administration and got splattered with a can of red paint, a harsh reminder of the danger she often found herself in.

After she married Hayden the couple moved to modest surroundings in Venice, California, before finally settling into a "working class" home in Santa Monica. In July 1973, Jane delivered her first son, named Troy O'Donovan Garity—the first name was after a Vietnamese patriot.

A Doll's House was Fonda's last full-length role for some years. She focused her remarkable energies on being a combination wife, mother, and activist; her political activity culminated in Hayden's narrowly unsuccessful bid for the United States Senate.

REVIEWS:

Andrew Sarris, *Village Voice.* Losey's direction was oriented more toward the house than the doll in this spatially expressionistic version of the play, and as a result there is more of a neurotic edge to the production. Fonda and Seyrig were reportedly concerned with adding additional feminist overtones, but the play is already too explicit for this kind of interpretive needlework. Fonda is quite good nonetheless.

Cinemundo: Nora, from the famous *A Doll's House,* is the perfect role for the independent-minded Jane Fonda. . . . She is at times too modern for the role, but her acting skill and her feminist courage make her Nora more striking than any before. Of course, Nora is not Jane Fonda, and luckily the Joseph Losey version of Ibsen's play, with modest additions from a modern writer, does not veer too far from the original. The supporting players are excellent and the house is more than a simple setting for the action. Despite the length of this movie, it is that too-rare blend of classic and entertainment.

Wyatt Cooper, *Talk:* In her first decent role in years, Jane Fonda scintillates as Nora in Henrik Ibsen's *A Doll's House,* a Joseph Losey production made on location in Ibsen's Norway. It is sad that there are two competing versions of this feminist classic, currently the subject of re- newed interest. The Fonda characterization is more multi-dimensional than that of Claire Bloom but, alas, Losey's *A Doll's House* was not—probably because of Ms. Fonda's politicking—released to theatres in North America. Instead, it bowed on ABC Television. This may not, however, be the curse it sounds, for even a low-rated TV offering usually attracts more viewers than most hit movies, and if any play of the last few hundred years deserves to reach a captive audience, it is *A Doll's House.*

Nora Sayre, *New York Times:* Those who believe that Nora would have returned to her particular prison will lose out to Jane Fonda and Joseph Losey: when this Nora leaves, it's forever.

Since we have two flawed versions of *A Doll's House* this year, it's exasperating to have to choose between the sets of mistakes that were

Jane Fonda confides her secrets and plans to a friend, Delphine Seyrig.

The plot begins to thicken, enmeshing the lives of Jane Fonda, David Warner,
Trevor Howard, and Delphine Seyrig.

made. . . . Claire Bloom plays Nora with such austerity that most of the play's emotional punch is lost. . . . The directors were wise to shun the fluffy, twittering Noras we've seen before, but they sacrificed the immaturity Ibsen gave her so that she might outgrow it. . . . The Losey script by David Mercer has been fattened with feeble lines and even short scenes that the old genius didn't write.

Of the two pictures, Losey's is the more ferociously flawed, and yet I recommend it over the other, for Jane Fonda's performance. Beforehand, it seemed fair to wonder if she could personify someone from the past; her voice, inflections and ways of moving have always seemed totally contemporary. (She may not smoke, but in *Klute* and elsewhere she sounded like at least two packs a day; no disrespect intended: the characters she plays are apt to be under severe pressures.) But once again she proves herself to be one of our finest actresses, and she's at home in the 1870s, a creature of that period as much as ours.

Dancing or laughing or worrying, eating macaroons, skating or suffering, Miss Fonda brings an emotional range to the part that Claire Bloom didn't: here is the ringing gaiety and the energy that the role demands. She can also be innocent without seeming stupid or silly—which is a traditional beartrap in this play.

Nora's habit of lying was played down in the Bloom version, and that made the character too noble. But it's exhilarating to watch what Fonda does with this reflex: she projects a person who is able to believe her own lies—such as pretending to have earned cash that she actually borrowed. . . . Gradually and subtly, we are given a portrait of Nora as a political prisoner—one who hasn't ever tasted the air outside the walls. And Miss Fonda is such a sensitive actress that we can even see the ideas taking root. . . .

179

Fonda indulges in a rare shopping trip.

Introduction to the Enemy

IPC Films, 1974. By Christine Burrill, Jane Fonda, Tom Hayden, Haskell Wexler, Bill Hayraus.

F.T.A. wasn't exactly a success, but this documentary about Vietnam was decidedly less so. It didn't receive a general release and went almost completely unreviewed. Its content may have been slightly less controversial than *F.T.A.*'s, but by the time it appeared, people had had their fill of Vietnam and the war had pretty much receded from the national consciousness.

Introduction to the Enemy was the first production of Fonda's IPC (Indochina Peace Campaign) Films, which went on to more commercial projects in the late seventies and early eighties, among them *The China Syndrome* and *Nine to Five.*

Here follows the complete *New York Times* review of the documentary.

REVIEW:

Nora Sayre, *New York Times:* Patience may never become one of our national characteristics. But we could take some lessons from the Vietnamese. Rebuilding and rebirth are the themes of *Introduction to the Enemy*, which was made collectively by Jane Fonda, Tom Hayden, Haskell Wexler, and others; it depicts their travel through North and South Vietnam last spring. The documentary is playing today at the First Avenue Screening Room. Anyone who was or is concerned with the war should see it—along with those who think that the war is over.

Throughout this quiet, modest film, in which scrap metal from American airplanes is made into bicycles, and an old man explains that he rebuilt his house 12 times (on five occasions after the French bombings, and seven times after the American raids) and misty green crops rise from filled-in craters, it is stressed that the Vietnamese do not hate Americans, that they want to know more about us. Again and again different Vietnamese citizens say that they distinguish between a population and its political leaders; they repeat that they do not blame Americans at large for the destruction of their country. Yet the wounds of their continuing experience are as tangible as the unexploded mine that goes off and kills a man during the filming.

The film seethes with small children; it seems quite amazing that there are so many Vietnamese children left alive, or that smiles of all ages should be turned toward the camera. Miss Fonda and Mr. Hayden function as unobtrusive guides. They journey from Hanoi to the South, crossing the demilitarized zone to the Quang Tri province. Miss Fonda interviews people about their work, asking why one chose to become an actress or a translator or a member of the resistance. The answers are thoughtful, decisive—as much personal as political.

Another recurrent theme is that Vietnam is one country—that the artificial division of the north and the south is not accepted by the Vietnamese. It's remarked that most families have relatives living in both areas; an editor adds, "The north and the south have always shared moments of joy as well as moments of sorrow and tragedy." Moreover, "American leaders are constantly reminding us that the bombing could be renewed." A very old man says he'd be happy to die if he could see one day of reunification.

Though the Paris Peace Arrangements have not been fulfilled, a restrained optimism surges through this documentary. The mood of the film is distilled when someone asserts that "The needs of peace are greater than the needs of war"—meaning that rebuilding schools and hospitals and homes and entire cities demands resources and energies that simply aren't available in wartime. All in all, this pensive and moving film serves as a chapter of our own education about the Vietnamese past and the rhythm of life in that country now.

The Bluebird

20th Century-Fox, 1976. Directed by George Cukor. Produced by Paul Maslansky. Screenplay by Hugh Whitemore and Alfred Hayes, based on the play by Maurice Maeterlinck.
PRINCIPAL CAST: Elizabeth Taylor, Jane Fonda, Ava Gardner, Cicely Tyson, Robert Morley, Will Geer, Mona Washbourne, and Nadejda Pavlova as the Bluebird.

IN 1975 JANE FONDA returned alone to the Soviet Union, which she once visited with Vadim. She went to do a small part in the first Soviet-American co-production, the expensive and time-consuming *The Bluebird,* starring Elizabeth Taylor in the remake of a former Shirley Temple vehicle. The play on which the film was based was a favorite with the Soviets.

Jane played the part of Night, appropriately costumed in black furs and velvet. Her lines were minimal: "I could have phoned in my part from Santa Monica!" Like some of the cast, she may have become disgusted with the continual breakdowns, interruptions, and inefficiency the moviemakers encountered in the Soviet Union. The crew was mostly Soviet, and the shooting

Cicely Tyson, as Cat, and Jane Fonda.

took more than one year, making this film one of the costliest movie debacles since *Cleopatra,* another Fox project starring Liz Taylor.

The Bluebird was more of a children's than an adults' story, based on the fairy-tale play by Maurice Maeterlinck. It didn't have enough universal appeal for moviegoers and was barely released in the U.S. It lost millions for Fox. Though the film was meant to foster goodwill between the American and Soviet movie industries, it strained cinematic relations and virtually ensured that there would be no further co-productions of this sort. Fonda escaped the fiasco unscathed, but in Hollywood this is considered the movie that nearly killed Taylor's career for good.

Admittedly, one of the things that attracted Jane to *The Bluebird* was the Soviet-American cooperation and the location shooting. "Ms. Fonda is more of a visitor than a typical Western star," declared one Soviet magazine. "She is eager to learn about our country and cement relationships between the two peoples, which *The Bluebird* will no doubt help."

The extremely basic plot was mostly an excuse, in this case, for displaying ornate Soviet sets, fancy American costumes, and a parade of major female stars in skimpy roles. Only Taylor had much to do, and she got the worst reviews, next to the film itself.

The plot tells of a fairy who asks two children with the unlikely names of Tyltyl and Myltyl to seek the Bluebird of Happiness. They set off on the long quest, aided by Taylor in various disguises. As Queen of Light, she gives the pair a magical hat encrusted with a magical diamond that allows the children to call upon the soul within each and every animate and inanimate object, like Bread, Milk, Water, Sugar, Fire, Cat, Dog, and Night. These personified souls graciously help Tyltyl and Myltyl, who end the unsuspenseful story by finding the Bluebird of Happiness in their own backyard (where else?).

REVIEWS:
Varieties magazine (U.S.S.R.): George Cukor, the American movie director who is most famous for guiding the great Greta Garbo, serves as director for *The Bluebird,* the first Soviet-American motion picture, for audiences around the world. It is a charming fairy tale, with interesting plot, beautiful visuals, and an international cast headed by English actress Elizabeth Taylor and including America's leading black actress, Cicely Tyson, and Jane Fonda, the actress who protested the imperialistic war in Vietnam.

Wyatt Cooper, *Talk: The Bluebird* is an enchanting story that was better served by Shirley Temple than Elizabeth Taylor. The focus of the tale has been changed from the children to the characters played by Miss Taylor in everything from witch's rags to peasant garb to opulent Edith Head creations. Ava Gardner also does a star turn as Avarice, with Cicely Tyson as Cat and Jane Fonda oddly cast as Night. . . . *Bluebird* drags at times, and it is hard to believe so many millions and so many months were expended on what is, after all, just another costume fairy tale.

London Movie Express: For a children's film, this one is top-heavy with middle-aged talents and archaic production values that do little to enhance the classical story which might otherwise have been enjoyed by all ages. . . . A mixture of Soviet ineptitude and the American belief that the grotesque expenditure of dollars can set anything a-right.

Vincent Canby, *New York Times.* [*The Bluebird*] was produced in the Soviet Union, mostly in Leningrad and environs, under the direction of an American . . . with American and English actors . . . with Soviet performers . . . with one English cameraman and one Soviet, and with dozens of Soviet technicians. . . . Yet as you watch it you keep seeing two films that want to compete but don't, everyone being too polite, accepting compromise, effectively neutered.

One of these films is blandly American, like the sort of processed cheese sold in jars that can later be used as water glasses. The other is dimly Russian but without any real Russian character, except for the sets, which aren't great. . . .

I'm afraid that I'm going to have to give away

Jane Fonda as Night in The Bluebird, *starring Elizabeth Taylor.*

the ending of the film; before the children learn that the Bluebird of Happiness is in their own backyard, they visit the kingdom of the past and the future, and the queendoms of night and luxury, at each stop learning some bit of wisdom. The film is not very old before you're longing to see a nice, self-absorbed Munchkin who wouldn't know an aphorism from a spitball.

Mr. Cukor . . . seems to have had less chance to direct in this case than to act as the goodwill ambassador who got his actors on and off the sets on time. The English-language screenplay . . . would try the inspirations of anyone. What could Mr. Cukor possibly have suggested to Miss Taylor to help her read a line like, "I am the light that makes men see/The radiance in reality?". . .

The Soviet cast members . . . are no better except when they are given a chance to dance. Nadejda Pavlova . . . dances the Bluebird, but we see a lot less of it than I'm sure the Soviet audiences will. Members of the Leningrad Kirov Ballet are also featured in other dances, all of which appear to have been abbreviated for our consumption. . . . We are also given several dreadful, disneyesque songs, including one stunner called "The Blue Haloo." . . . Then there are all those bluebirds: Some look like blackbirds and some are simply pigeons dyed blue.

Hugh Whitemore and Alfred Hayes are credited with the screenplay but when Miss Fonda comes on, dressed in modified *Barbarella* gear as Night, I began to think she had written her own lines. Frets Night for no reason that has anything to do with the kiddie-quest for the Bluebird, "What times we live in. I don't understand these last few years." Night sounds as if she had been moonlighting in the America of the Nixon administration.

This kind of co-production does nothing for either party. The élan of the American film talents, particularly Cukor's, is wasted, perhaps inhibited, while the talents of the Soviet participants, particularly those of the Kirov Ballet, are seen so fleetingly that the film could just as easily have been shot in Hoboken.

Jane Fonda and her cohorts help Todd Lookinland in his search for the Bluebird of Happiness.

184

Fun with Dick and Jane

Columbia, 1977. Directed by Ted Kotcheff. Produced by Peter Bart and Max Palevsky. Screenplay by David Giler, Jerry Belson and Mordecai Richler. Story by Gerald Gaiser.
PRINCIPAL CAST: George Segal, Jane Fonda, Ed McMahon, Hank Garcia, Dick Gautier.

DICK IS AN AEROSPACE executive who is laid off during a sag in the economy. He gets the bad news from his boss, whom he doesn't know is involved in a potential bribery scandal. Unfortunately, Dick and his wife, Jane, have been living beyond their means, mostly on credit, and Dick is overqualified for other jobs. Jane, on the other hand, is underqualified, for she has always been a housewife. Dick goes on welfare, credi-

tors move in on the beleaguered family, and their son plaintively asks, "Are we going to be poor, like the Waltons?"

Jane tries to make ends meet, sacrificing the family's membership in the Book-of-the-Month Club, letting the pool go unheated, etc. She next tries a job but gets fired. Things are getting more desperate, and when Jane finds herself in accidental possession of stolen money, Dick gets

Jane Fonda as Jane, a suburban housewife.

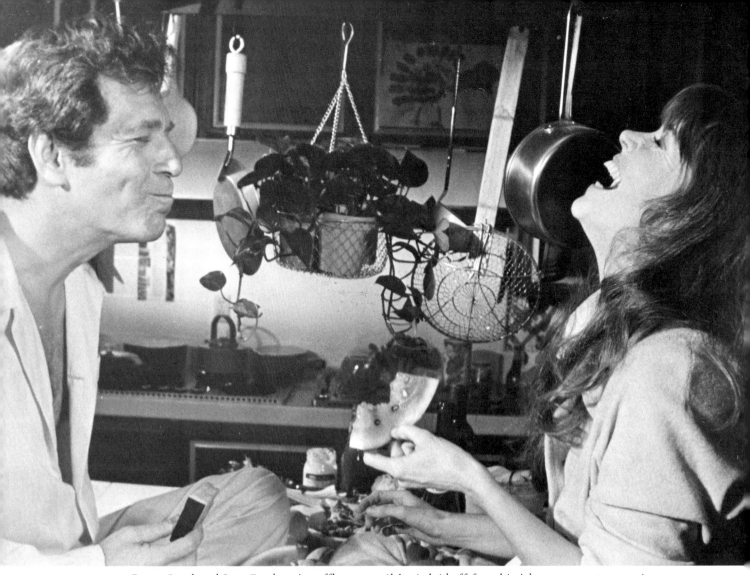

George Segal and Jane Fonda enjoy affluence until he is laid off from his job as an aerospace engineer.

the idea of supplementing their income by robbing drugstores, supermarkets, and even the phone company—the latter to the admiring applause of fed-up customers. Jane accompanies and guides Dick through various comically profitable situations. Eventually, the happy-go-lucky couple goes for the big bucks in his former boss's slush fund, and they manage to get away with it. They live, one presumes, happily—and guiltlessly—ever after.

Fun with Dick and Jane was Fonda's first hit in seven years and her first full-length role in more than four. It marked her comeback to full-time, mainstream acting, and its success enabled her

to go on to more serious projects, which made her a bigger star than ever and certainly a more respected actress. For her return to films she chose a comedy, to "show that I could still be pretty and still had a sense of humor." Finding a leading man for this recession-related comedy wasn't easy, but George Segal was willing and eager to work with the controversial actress. He asked for and got first billing.

Even so, it was Jane's victory, and as the film became a huge hit, the publicity raved, "America Loves Jane Fonda Again." Most of the reviews were favorable or mild, but most expressed the opinion that Fonda had been away too long. The film's only sour note was a tasteless bathroom scene that caused some unfavorable comment. A few critics, like Rona Barrett, rebuked the ending, which let the couple go unpunished for the larceny they had committed—it was a big change from the old days of obligatory retribution in movies.

What had kept Jane from finding more work in the mid-seventies? According to her, it was an "unofficial" boycott by producers, directors, and actors not to mention studio executives and theater owners, who didn't wish to provide work for an actress accused of treason. She had been widely denounced as a traitor following her first visit to North Vietnam, and a few groups had attempted to have her deported and her films officially boycotted. Hollywood shunned her, talk shows were reluctant to have her as a guest, and even fan magazines avoided using her name, but after *Fun with Dick and Jane* everything was all right again, for the most part.

A few years later, when she was named Female Star of the World by the National Association of Theatre Owners, she was asked on a talk show who the people were who had tried to prevent her from working again. She answered candidly, "The same guys who are giving me this award."

REVIEWS:

Motion Picture: Sooner or later, someone had to make a comedy picture about inflation, recession, lay-offs and credit card-living. It figures that ever-relevant Jane Fonda would choose just such a picture for her return to the silver screen. She is excellent playing, basically, herself, and she gets the chance to sport several changes of snappy wardrobe, plus different wigs and hairstyles. One scene in the john could have been left on the shelf, but apart from that, *Fun with Dick and Jane* is a comedy the whole family can enjoy together, as long as the ending isn't taken seriously.

London Movie Express: George Segal stars in yet another of the kind of comedies which have made him a box office star. Had he followed through with the potential he displayed in *Who's Afraid of Virginia Woolf?* he might have become

Segal's joblessness means that he and Fonda must cut corners and adjust to a less-fashionable image.

187

a leading dramatic actor. Jane Fonda, by contrast, appears to be trying to change from stern tragedienne to bouncy comedienne, and is ill at ease in the latter role. She does well enough, but the brittleness shows, and after the demanding roles she has weathered, she should hold out for more challenging material, now that she is one of America's few legitimate thespians.

Wyatt Cooper, *Talk*: I wanted to like *Fun with Dick and Jane*. The titles were cute. "See Jane play." "Run, Dick, Run." But from there on it was downhill. . . . George Segal loses his job as an aerospace executive and, since he is overqualified for any sort of job that's available to him, he is amazed and horrified to find himself in a kind of land-of-no-return. His wife, Jane Fonda, tries to help but there's not much she can do to support the lifestyle they've been enjoying. The situation is a valid one and, in fact, a good situation for comedy. Being poor is probably much harder on the recently prosperous than on those more accustomed to it. Coping with it takes experience.

Segal and Fonda set out on a desperate career as bank robbers and the two actors get the style right. Fonda has a pert manner that is most engaging, though she's saddled with some impossible scenes (for instance, the one in which she's supposed to fail miserably and clumsily at modeling in a restaurant, when any fool can see that Fonda would be superb at anything she chose to do). . . . There's a delicious scene in which the men from the nursery company roll up and haul away the unpaid-for lawn. But the scriptwriters pushed too hard and the strain showed, which is death to comedy.

Vincent Canby, *New York Times: Fun with Dick and Jane* . . . is a deceptively sunny, sometimes uproariously funny comedy about the bad taste, vulgarity and awful aimlessness of a certain kind of middle-class American affluence. Buried not very deeply within the film, there is a small flaw. We are asked to like and to sympathize with Dick and Jane . . . and we do like them enormously, even though the characters are completely dedicated to maintaining all-wrong values. In this respect, the film seems to want to

After their first success at robbery, Jane Fonda and George Segal turn to crime to support their nuclear family.

189

George Segal admires wife Jane Fonda, who fingers some of their illegal funds.

Segal and Fonda plan another colorful heist.

stand on both sides of the fence at once, to take credit for having a social conscience while not really honoring it.

I never have trouble remembering that Miss Fonda is a fine dramatic actress but I'm surprised all over again every time I see her do comedy with the mixture of comic intelligence and abandon she shows here. One sequence in particular, in which she makes a botch of an attempt at fashion modeling in a crowded restaurant at lunchtime, is a nearly priceless piece of modern slapstick.

190

Fonda and Segal have the last laugh when they prove that crime really does pay.

Julia

20th Century-Fox, 1977. Directed by Fred Zinnemann. Produced by Richard Roth. Screenplay by Alvin Sargent, based on the book Pentimento, *by Lillian Hellman.*

PRINCIPAL CAST: Jane Fonda, Vanessa Redgrave, Jason Robards, Maximilian Schell, Hal Holbrook, Meryl Streep.

THE RELATIONSHIP OF Lillian Hellman and Julia is told through flashbacks and key episodes in their eventful young lives, spanning two decades and two continents. The plot traces Lillian's evolution as a writer, nurtured by the tender, if demanding, presence of Dashiell Hammett. It also recounts Julia's alienation from her ancient, wealthy family and her development into an anti-Nazi fighter and martyr. Julia's social and political convictions barely touch the passive Lil-

Jane Fonda, as Lillian Hellman in Julia, *is called upon to perform a dangerous assignment for her friend.*

lian, who loses touch with her friend and achieves fame with her first play, *The Children's Hour.*

While visiting Paris, Lillian tries to get in touch with Julia, who has been studying in Vienna with Sigmund Freud. Discovering that her friend has been badly injured by a group of Nazi thugs, Lillian rushes to Julia's bedside. The two have a tender reunion, though Julia is too badly hurt to speak above a whisper. Lillian returns to the hospital the next day, only to find that Julia has been spirited away by the underground.

Their next encounter is their last. Back in Paris, Lillian accepts a request, on behalf of the cause and Julia, to smuggle fifty thousand dollars into Berlin in a conspicuous (and therefore unsuspected) wool hat. After much peril and suspense, the women meet in a smoke-filled café in the film's most praised scene. They carry on a moving, low-key conversation, the exchange is made, and Lillian Hellman returns to everyday life, finally aware of the meaning of courage.

Julia was shot mainly in France and England. Detractors quickly nicknamed it *Reds in Bed.* Much comment was made of the scene in which Lillian, filled with admiration for the stately, obstreperous Julia, impetuously uttered the first screen "I love you" from one woman to another in years. Some of the publicity was negative, suggestive, or downright destructive. To some, it was significant that Hellman was the author of *The Children's Hour,* a play with a Lesbian theme. Fonda and Redgrave ignored the snide comments, and Jane proclaimed, "Oh, to be able to play in scenes with another woman! People will see a movie about women who think and who care for each other. . . . In every other movie I've ever done and most movies I see where there's a woman, she's either falling in or out of love or worried that she's going to lose a man. She's always defined in relationship to a man."

Jane was glowing in her praise for Redgrave, though she admitted that as a "progressive Democrat" she didn't see eye to eye with her co-star's Trotskyite politics. They handled their differences by not discussing politics. Fonda opined that Redgrave was the best performer she'd ever

Budding playwright Lillian Hellman is given moral support and technical encouragement by Dashiell Hammett, played by Jason Robards.

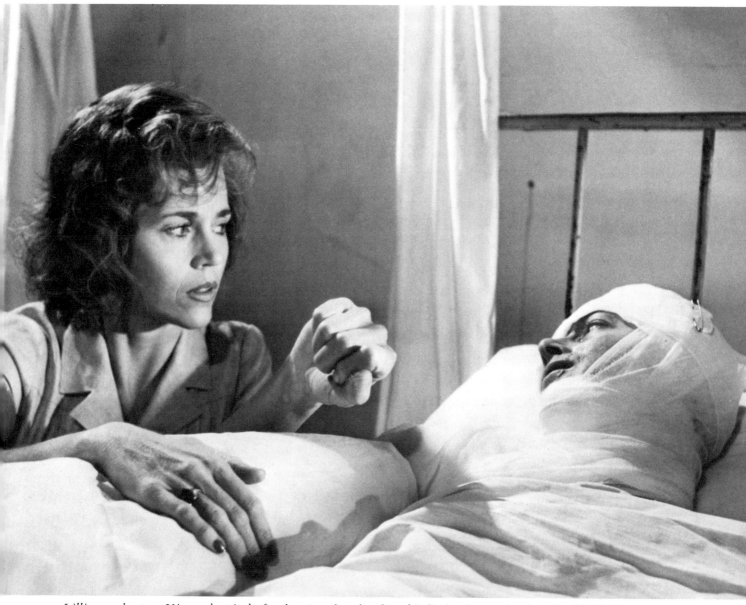

Lillian rushes to a Vienna hospital after hearing that her friend Julia has been seriously injured by fascists.

worked with, even better than Brando. "In the goodbye scene we'd stand there and before the shooting began she'd say things to me like, 'Lily, I want you to be brave, I don't want you to give up on your writing. . . .' I looked at her hands and I started to cry because she's got these huge hands that are very moving to me."

Of the actresses' comparative techniques, Fred Zinnemann stated, "With Vanessa you don't feel there's any work, any effort. Her act-

ing just flows. With Jane there's a lot of pains-taking detail and work. Fonda has one quality she shares with Porfirio Díaz, the old Mexican dictator, and Louis B. Mayer, the old MGM dictator—she can cry at will and be totally convincing."

Jane visited Lillian Hellman in Martha's Vineyard. Instead of discussing the script they ended up defending the cottage from an impending hurricane. They cut flowers, took mirrors off

Young Lillian Hellman, living and frolicking on the New England shore, prepares to write her first play,
The Children's Hour.

195

the walls, and fastened down storm windows. The hurricane didn't hit the area. Fonda did pick up certain mannerisms, however, noting the way Hellman crossed herself and said, *"Oy vey!"* at the same time.

Eventually she decided against doing a broad impersonation: "Lillian is a homely woman, and yet she moves as if she were Marilyn Monroe. She sits with her legs apart, with her satin underwear partly showing. She's a very sexual, sensual woman. That's fine for Lillian, but it wouldn't look right if I did it. So I played her more ascetic than she really is." The film contained nary a centimeter of cleavage and little romantic interplay between Hellman and Hammett. Perhaps *Barbarella* was still too close for comfort.

Making *Julia* meant three and a half months away from home; she had to leave behind Tom and Troy, but Vanessa stayed with Vadim in

Paris, while Jane—never fond of hotels—rented a twentieth-story flat in the futuristic Tour Espace 2000 (Space Tower 2000). This time around she assiduously avoided the Parisian social whirl, begging off numerous invitations by explaining that this was her most important film, which meant hard work. She reread the script several times, suggested changes to her director, and spent long nights with Redgrave discussing the interpretation and motivation of the characters, the faithfulness of the script to the memoir, and fine details of their performances.

After Hellman viewed the final product at a New York screening she endorsed it fully and congratulated Fonda on her work. This came as a complete surprise. "I don't see how she could like it," said Fonda. "Here were the two most important relationships of her life—with Julia and her lover, Dashiell Hammett, played by Ja-

Hal Holbrook, as one of Lillian's witty society friends in Manhattan,
keeps Lillian's mind off the growing troubles in 1930s Europe.

Maximilian Schell, as a member of the anti-fascist underground, asks Lillian to undertake a perilous journey on Julia's behalf.

son Robards—passing through the prisms of another writer, a director, actors. Given all that, I'm amazed at her response." But no one else was.

REVIEWS:

Norma McLain Stoop, *After Dark: Julia* is a spellbinding movie whose every frame exudes good taste, as did the story on which it is based. Directed by Fred Zinnemann and produced by Richard Roth . . . it is a courageous film about courage, about two of the hundreds of kinds of courage of which human beings are capable. The choices made by Julia and Lillian are the fabric of this engrossing film. Alvin Sargent's excellent screenplay, so faithful to Hellman's story, combined with the depth of Redgrave and Fonda's immersion in their roles, constantly pull the viewer into the action, into an agonizing, "What would I have done? Of what am *I* capable?"

Jane Fonda is so good as Lillian that it is almost embarrassing to watch her—one feels like a trespasser in the privacy of a life. Whether throwing her typewriter out the window of a Long Island beach cottage in despair at the progress of her play, holding the bruised hand of bandage-swathed Julia in a hospital in Vienna, slapping the face of a drunken New York friend who questions her relationship with Julia, trying to accustom herself to intrigue on the German border in the Hitler era or loving and screaming at the patient, supportive Hammett, she never

197

loses a radiance born not only from talent but from self. Fonda gives what is unquestionably the finest film performance of any woman this year.

Lillian Hellman's reminiscence of "what was there for me once, what is there for me now" has been made into a paragon of a movie that illuminates loyalty, love, self-doubt and self-sacrifice with the electricity of its passionate commitment to excellence.

Time: On paper, *Julia* sounds like an exemplary American film. In sharp contrast to most current big-budget movies it trades in serious ideas rather than comic book fantasies and it even has the guts to buck Hollywood's long-standing embargo on heroines by starring two strong, intelligent women who care about other things than men. . . . *Julia*'s problems trace back to its source, a Lillian Hellman story that appeared in her 1973 memoir *Pentimento*. Whatever its virtues, *Julia* is short on plot and jumps around in time.

The film works up some steam when it is recounting the central anecdote of the original story, a scary 1937 train ride in which Hellman smuggles $50,000 to Julia and her anti-fascist comrades in Berlin. Director Zinnemann *(High Noon)* brings a Graham Greenesque sense of intrigue to this adventure and he sets up a powerful climactic scene. When Hellman finally arrives at a smoky Berlin café to deliver the loot, her terse, hurried conversation with Julia sums up everything the film has been trying to say about friendship, political commitment and growing up. Simultaneously the two star performances crystallize.

Harriet Lyons and Susan Braudy, *Ms:* Like a spring romance, *Julia* promises a heady mix: at long last a movie about a loving and complex friendship between two women; a screenplay based on a chapter from the celebrated *Pentimento;* the return of Jane Fonda in a major dramatic role; plus the strong presence of British actress and activist Vanessa Redgrave. . . . We are treated to outstanding performances by Fonda and Redgrave as they recreate two

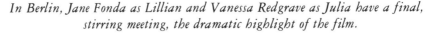

In Berlin, Jane Fonda as Lillian and Vanessa Redgrave as Julia have a final, stirring meeting, the dramatic highlight of the film.

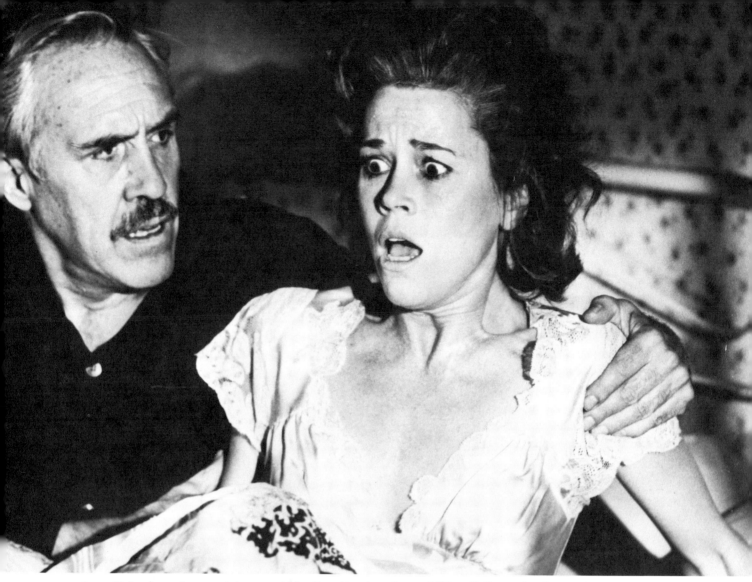

Jason Robards comforts a nightmare-ridden Jane Fonda, who, as Lillian Hellman, has been trying in vain to locate the baby daughter of her late friend Julia, a political martyr.

women who are strong, solitary, dedicated to ideas and ideals. Fred Zinnemann's direction and Alvin Sargent's script offer a sympathetic view of each woman's independence and priorities.

The friendship on the screen is flattened. Zinnemann has not sought cinematic equivalents for the emotional subtleties in the memoir. He has instead trained an almost exploitive camera on the sexual current between the two women. Zinnemann fortunately leaves Lillian and Julia's final meeting intact. Here, the emotion doesn't elude him. Julia, knowing she may never see her friend again, offers an exquisite tribute to Lillian's characteristic anger. "Don't let people talk you out of it. It may be uncomfortable for them

but it's valuable to you. It's what made you bring the money in today."

Zinnemann misses a gut level of understanding among the women. Although he accepts Lillian and Julia's integrity and choices as individuals, he cannot bring himself to trust Hellman's platonic rendering of their friendship. In his hands the friendship is little more than an extended teenage crush. *Julia*—by far the most interesting film about women to come along in a while—is, alas, not the woman's film we were promised.

Jack Kroll, *Newsweek:* "I love you, Julia." It's the ultimate movie cliché line, heard a million times with only the name changing through the alphabet from Arlene to Zenobia. And in the new film *Julia* it's uttered as it so often has been on a romantic hillside, with nature beaming down on two beautiful young people in the sweetness of their bond. But in *Julia* it is spoken by one woman to another, and that is likely to make it the most significant line of the year. The love that Lillian is expressing for Julia is the deep friendship of one woman for another, a relationship that films have notoriously been ignoring while finding new variations on the male buddyhood that made Redford and Newman the fun couple of the decade. *Julia* supposedly signals a new deal for women in films, in which they'll no longer be satellites to men but suns and stars in their own right.

When Richard Roth acquired the rights to *Pentimento* every actress who was ambulatory went after the roles—Lillian, the budding playwright, and Julia, her childhood friend who rebelled against her aristocratic family to become a martyr in the anti-fascist underground. But no actresses could be more appropriate, professionally and symbolically, to play these roles than Jane Fonda and Vanessa Redgrave, both remarkable performers, both controversial women who insisted on playing highly visible roles in left-wing politics. In *Julia* Fonda and Redgrave are close to perfection and the pathos and power of friendship they create is the movie's great virtue.

Julia is moving in its glowing commitment to the power of friendship. The climax of the film is Lillian's last meeting with Julia in a Berlin restaurant. Fonda and Redgrave create a heartbreaking interplay of emotions without a taint of sentimentality. Lillian and Julia will never see each other again but in the paranoid air of Nazi Germany in 1937 they can't fully express their feelings. A friendship is being immolated before our eyes, and suddenly Fascism seems to be anything that thwarts human beings from growing with and for one another.

Coming Home

United Artists, 1978. Directed by Hal Ashby. Produced by Jerome Hellman. Screenplay by Waldo Salt and Robert C. Jones. Story by Nancy Dowd.
PRINCIPAL CAST: Jane Fonda, Jon Voight, Bruce Dern, Penelope Milford, Robert Carradine.

Coming Home chronicled the relationships and changes in three characters, played by Fonda, Jon Voight, and Bruce Dern. Sally Hyde is an unliberated military wife striving to "look like Jackie Kennedy" and please her captain-husband, a man who firmly believes woman's place is in the home. When Captain Hyde is sent to Vietnam Sally is on her own for the first time. To make herself useful she volunteers to work in a hospital ward for disabled veterans, specifically paraplegics. Luke Martin is an embittered vet whose stint in Vietnam cost him the use of his legs. He is surly and sour until he becomes friends with Sally, a former high school class-

Jane Fonda in her second Oscar-winning role, as Sally Hyde.

mate. The two expand their mutual horizons and bring romance and understanding into each other's lives.

When the officer comes home he is as embittered as Luke, though for different reasons. His leg has been superficially wounded, and he has been decorated. When he discovers that his wife is having an affair with another man, something snaps inside him, and during a confrontation with the couple he threatens them with a bayonet. He finally backs down, and Sally agrees to stop seeing Luke for the sake of her marriage. The captain shortly commits suicide by swimming into the sea.

Coming Home was begun when Fonda commissioned a female writer to do a Vietnam screenplay. Two new writers were later brought in, and producer Jerome Hellman and Bruce Gilbert, Jane's partner in IPC Films, joined the fold. Englishman John Schlesinger *(Midnight Cowboy)*

was set to direct but departed amicably after finding the material too alien to his background. He was replaced by Hal Ashby *(Shampoo)*. So far, Fonda was the only star in the project. Hellman declared, "We liked each other right away, and we understood each other. She required very few conditions, but one of the things she did extract was a promise that I would make a concerted effort to get a racially and sexually balanced crew."

A top box-office star was sought for the male lead, to offset the grim nature of the story. Pacino, Nicholson, and Stallone were all offered the part but declined. Voight had been considered for the role of the husband, but after becoming involved with the project he campaigned to play the paraplegic vet. He got the plum role, and Bruce Dern, long stereotyped in sadistic roles, was chosen for the husband. Jon had participated in the antiwar movement and

Vi Munson (Penelope Milford) becomes Sally's best friend. Vi's boyfriend and Sally's husband are fighting in Vietnam.

was a friend of Fonda, who was instrumental in helping him land the role, even though he'd fallen from box-office grace since his *Midnight Cowboy* days.

Taped and written material was gathered and sifted through several times until the project could wait no longer. "The gun we had to our heads," said Hellman, "was Fonda's film commitments. She had gone off to do *Julia* and then after our picture was scheduled to make a film for Alan Pakula." Shooting proceeded smoothly, a rewarding experience for all concerned. The ending, however, presented a problem. Hellman explained, "When we started out there was a very violent ending, but none of us liked it. For a film about the consequences of violence to end with violence seemed wrong. Finally we reached some conclusions. The paraplegic was going to survive; there was no question in any of our minds, particularly after we

had met the paraplegics. Jane's character was a survivor. But we felt that Bruce Dern's character was so dedicated to one way of seeing things that if he could no longer depend upon that value system, he couldn't live."

No one ventured to prophesy the reaction to *Coming Home,* for Vietnam was an untried movie subject and the R-rated film featured a realistic treatment of paraplegics, heretofore completely ignored by Hollywood. As for its stars, Voight and Dern had little box-office weight and Fonda herself was not yet a guarantor of respectable profits. Protests from veterans' groups, handicapped and otherwise, were likely, and some studio executives feared audiences would stay away in droves from anything even remotely connected with Vietnam. *American Film,* the magazine of the American Film Institute, described the progress of *Coming Home:*

Sally meets disabled veteran Luke Martin (Jon Voight) in the veterans' hospital, and they become romantically involved.

Fonda and Voight enjoying a meal.

A few weeks before *Coming Home* opened in Washington, D.C., producer Jerome Hellman arranged a private screening in the city for what he called "my toughest audience." He flew in from California to attend it. The audience included representatives of veterans' groups, some of whom were not well disposed toward the antiwar activity of Jane Fonda. . . . After the screening Hellman stepped before the group and waited for a response. . . . It was warm, favorable, moving. One young man in a wheelchair, groping for words, said the film had caught the experience of the paraplegic. Hellman stayed an hour longer than he planned; he left with one paraplegic marine's grudging good wishes to Jane Fonda.

The actress later explained that she and Bruce Gilbert

go about developing movies backwards. Usually you start with a character, but we start with what we want to say. Then we figure out a story, because no matter how right or justified you feel, unless you interest people, it's not getting across. . . . How does a woman like Sally Hyde move, dress, talk? That's what I want to know. What enhances a role a thousandfold is that the degree to which I can render that woman real has a whole political implication for me personally, because those are the kinds of people who hate me, who thought I was a traitor.

Remember, there are still a lot of people out there who would like to see me dead.

When government cooperation was sought to film *Coming Home* at the Long Beach Veterans Administration Hospital it was flatly refused. Not only the VA, but the army, navy, marine corps, and national guard all turned down Fonda and company. Shooting took place instead at a hospital for spinal-cord injuries in Downey, California. Only after *Coming Home* opened did the VA cautiously approve the film—unofficially, of course. The movie was screened for a representative of the President's Committee on Employment of the Handicapped. This representative informed Hellman that it was "a very important film," the first time she had "seen a disabled person on the screen dealt with as a complete human being."

Coming Home won Oscars for writers Nancy Dowd, Waldo Salt, and Robert C. Jones, as well as for Jon Voight and Jane Fonda. When Jane was nominated for best actress for the fourth time in 1979 it was no contest. She was rewarded as much for her contribution to high-quality films in general and for striking a responsive cord with movie-goers, as for her role as

Sally visits her husband, Bob (Bruce Dern), in Hong Kong, and they do the town.

Sally Hyde. Her second win was announced with a triumphant whoop of glee by fellow activist Shirley MacLaine, and Fonda's level of enthusiasm was far greater and more visible than in 1972. She delivered a touching acceptance speech, simultaneously rendering it in American Sign Language, "my way of acknowledging over fourteen million Americans who are deaf."

Best actor Jon Voight (his first win) was even more emotional, his eyes clouding with tears as he paid tribute to Jane, his co-star and friend, "whose great dignity as a human being is very moving to me."

REVIEWS:
Stephen Farber, *New West:* Despite a garbled conclusion the relationship between Jane Fonda

and Jon Voight made this the most unexpectedly moving love story of the year. A special word of praise for Fonda, the finest actress now working in America.

Time: The movie is about those unfortunate Americans who could not escape the war's deadly grasp: the men who fought in Vietnam and the women they left behind. . . . Though the illicit affair of a beautiful woman and a cripple is

potentially mawkish stuff, Ashby does not allow his story to become overly sentimental. He does not view the couple's relationship as a panacea for all their emotional problems and he refuses to shy away from harsh detail. . . . Fonda, though unconvincing in Sally's pre-liberation scenes, ultimately brings her character's horrifying internal conflicts to the surface. At such moments *Coming Home* reminds us of the choices everybody made during those harrowing war

Home from the war, Bob receives a medal for bravery while a proud Sally poses with him.

years—and of the price the nation paid thereafter.

Charles Champlin, *Los Angeles Times:* Hal Ashby's stateside drama of the Vietnam war years was at one level an unusual triangular love story but the relationships themselves were consequences of the war and they also reflected fundamental changes in American perceptions of the war. The portrayals by Jon Voight as a paraplegic veteran, Jane Fonda as a military wife and Bruce Dern as her marine husband were as fine as any in the year. There were those who felt the love play overwhelmed the considerations of war. But despite an overexplicit songtrack and some moments when the story in fact became a sermon, the movie effectively translated a changed national consciousness into credible and touching personal terms. It conveyed a loss not of innocence but of naïveté, passing through anger into compassion touched with hope.

Gloria Emerson, *Ms:* I went to see *Coming Home* determined to be the coldest of critics, to note clearly all its defects and not to be swayed by my immense respect for Jane Fonda, who so much wanted this movie to be made. As Sally Hyde, wife of a marine captain (Bruce Dern), she plays a very narrow and nice woman who still teases and straightens her hair, a creature of the '50s although the year is 1968. Suddenly left on her own in California after her husband goes to Vietnam, she volunteers to work in a Veterans Administration hospital where the war casualties are pouring in. Nothing can ever be the same again for her. Here she meets a former high school classmate in the ward for men with spinal cord injuries (Jon Voight) and they become friends and lovers although Fonda does not want to leave her husband, a dull and overbearing fellow.

There is not a careless, maudlin moment—or any of the fake footage of staged firefights that so weakened two other Vietnam films, *Heroes* and *The Boys in Company C.* It is not a film composed only of sequences of pain and grief. Sometimes there is surprising humor and im-

mense sweetness. Moments like this: Voight, confined forever to a wheelchair, tries to tell Fonda that he is still himself. "I don't even have a chair in my dreams," he says, remembering how as a small boy he loved to jump very high and would leave his fingerprints on the kitchen ceiling.

Jack Kroll, *Newsweek:* Fonda's character undergoes the greatest transformation. Starting out as a do-good volunteer at the hospital who's capable of asking the paralyzed Voight, "Why are you so cynical, Luke?" she winds up angrily lecturing the other military wives who'd rather write sports items for the base paper than write about the soldiers' problems. She falls in love with Voight, lets her hair go curly and has her first satisfying sexual experience despite his paralysis.

Much of this is touching, sincere, compassionate and wryly funny. . . . All those performances blend intensity and modesty into a sensitively inflected realism that gives the film integrity. . . . There's a lot to admire in *Coming Home.* Haskell Wexler's cinematography is masterly, a luminous dramatizing of detail. The background music, numbers by the Beatles, Dylan, Richie Havens, the Rolling Stones, etc., sharply reminds you of the reality reflected by the rock music of the '60s.

Playboy: This is no tearjerker about agonizing rehabilitation. . . . *Coming Home* is emotionally rich, romantic and played for the adult market by Jane and Jon, whose scenes together produce the kind of chemistry that prompts movie-goers to start lining up around the block. . . . When Dern comes home—an embittered would-be hero who is decorated for accidentally shooting himself in the leg—the FBI gets into the act. What has been until now a gripping personal drama suddenly becomes a federal case. We are informed that Jane still loves her husband but it's not easy to believe she has ever been wholly serious about Dern, bearing down rather hard in his role as a possessive macho pig whose concepts of wife, honor and country were all born on the Fourth of July.

Comes a Horseman

United Artists, 1978. Directed by Alan J. Pakula. Produced by Gene Kirkwood and Dan Paulson.
Screenplay by Dennis Lynton Clark.
PRINCIPAL CAST: James Caan, Jane Fonda, Jason Robards, Richard Farnsworth, George Grizzard.

"THE WEST WAS WON by men and challenged by a woman," read the ads for *Comes a Horseman,* a "new" kind of western set in Montana immediately after World War II. What made it new was that its central character was a woman—not just any woman, but Jane Fonda. As Ella Connors, she was determined to hold on to her land in the face of corrupt corporate interests headed by ruthless cattle tycoon Jason Robards (as Ewing), who was also an old flame of hers.

Along comes James Caan (as Frank), a war vet without any plans. He agrees to work for Connors and later with her, supporting her in her fight with Robards and companies (oil companies are also mixed up in this). Several explosions and a cattle stampede later, the pair falls in love, Connors lets her hair down (literally and figuratively), and the partners courageously face the challenges confronting them. Ewing is killed, Connors retains her land, for the time being, and the sun sets on the western frontier.

Another ad for *Comes a Horseman* (originally

Jane Fonda hires James Caan to work on her ranch.

Caan and Fonda rope a steer.

titled *Comes a Horseman Wild and Free*) proclaimed, "She was a strong as the land for which she fought. And as vulnerable." However, this was one of Fonda's less vulnerable roles. Through most of the film Ella was distinctly unglamorous, untalkative, un-made-up, a hardworking ranchwoman (originally written as a good-time girl, before Jane entered the project). Ella was as unlike Barbarella and the other Vadim vamps as possible. Fonda stole the show, and despite a first-billed role, James Caan didn't make much of an impact.

Neither, for that matter, did the film itself, which was a bit dull and unrelenting in the starkness of the landscape and the people inhabiting it. *Horseman* didn't bomb at the box office, but it earned less money and praise than Fonda's last two movies. It was the third teaming for her and Jason Robards, the previous ones being *Any Wednesday* and *Julia,* for the latter of which he won a supporting Oscar, as did, of course, Vanessa Redgrave. It was also Fonda's second outing with Alan J. Pakula, the first being *Klute.*

The director explained, "The picture is a return to heroes, to people who are not smaller than life." As for the elements that decided Pakula on helming the project, "Another attraction was the chance to explore a woman in the American West as a heroic character. In most westerns the woman is in a calico dress, running after the hero on the horse saying, 'Nothing is worth dying for,' or she's a gun-toting Calamity Jane. The idea of dealing with a heroine in the West, very much a woman yet willing to fight with the same passion as men, was a great attraction. I thought there was no one better than Jane Fonda to represent that kind of strong yet vulnerable American woman."

Comes a Horseman also profiled the work of the ranchpeople played by its stars, and Jane had to learn to lasso, ride herd, and perform minor stunts and actual ranchwork. She'd learned to ride as a child but was instructed in the finer points of rounding up cattle and making her way through a stampede by a stuntwoman, whom she praised highly. As for Caan, he was already a rodeo nut and a would-be cowboy.

"I am fascinated with telling stories about work," continued Pakula. "I guess you could say *Klute* is a story about work. *Comes a Horseman* is a story of ranching, in a certain way, even though hopefully it works on other levels. But getting the ranching right was very important to me. If Jane Fonda and Jimmy Caan had not worked as hard as they did to get the ranching right, there would have been no picture."

REVIEWS:

Richard Grenier, *Cosmopolitan: Comes a Horseman* is another kind of western entirely. Here, we are in a grim, stark world of deep hatreds, primitive living conditions, desperate economics. Faultlessly, Jane Fonda plays a tough, independent small ranch owner and cowgirl, with firm stride and wind-weathered face.... Since the story takes place in the 20th century, the external agency that sets everything flying is not gold or the railroads, but oil. Director Pakula knows how to make a verbally exciting movie when he wants to, but the dialogue of *Horseman* is sparse, hard-bitten and so laconic that it can be hard to follow. The Land. Strong, silent men. Strong, silent women. The West according to Alan Pakula. But Jane Fonda, too, has a vision for us, I think. Women, be strong! In strength lies happiness! That's the way I read Jane Fonda.

McCall's: The tender relationship between Jane Fonda and James Caan almost redeems this dull and draggy post–World War II western about Fonda's fight to keep her ranch from the murderous (and shooting and knifing) cattle baron (Jason Robards). Despite its tedium, I like the movie because the Fonda-Caan relationship begins with their working together and grows into mutual respect and tenderness, out of which eventually springs sexual desire. It's refreshing to see a movie in which sexual attraction depends upon more than good looks or a fast line.

Circus: Jane Fonda, James Caan and Jason Robards star in a 1940s western about a woman trying to keep her farm from being bought by a bad guy and some unscrupulous oil men. It's hard to

Jane Fonda and James Caan ride herd on her property, beneath which lie large oil fields.

figure this film. It is beautiful (filmed in Colorado), amusing (great flashes of humor) and even exciting (wonderful action photography). But somehow it doesn't add up. Maybe because James Caan swallows so many of his dialogue lines; maybe it's because the plot is time-worn; maybe it's because there seem to be so many loose ends in the story. Whatever it is, it reduces the film to a quirkily interesting but unsuccessful work.

Horizon: Jane Fonda and Jason Robards, who were coupled as the lovers Lillian Hellman and Dashiell Hammett in last year's *Julia,* find themselves on opposite sides of the fence in *Comes a*

Horseman, a western set in Montana after World War II. Fonda stars as a rancher whose home on the range is threatened by a ruthless cattle baron—is there any other kind of cattle baron in the movies?—played by Robards. James Caan also appears as Fonda's partner in affairs, business as well as romance. . . . The film was directed by Alan J. Pakula, who examined greed on a much larger scale in his last film, *All the President's Men.*

Time: Clark's story is a hybrid of *The Rainmaker* and the collected works of Larry McMurtry *(Hud, The Last Picture Show)*. He tells of two antagonistic small-time ranchers, a tomboy

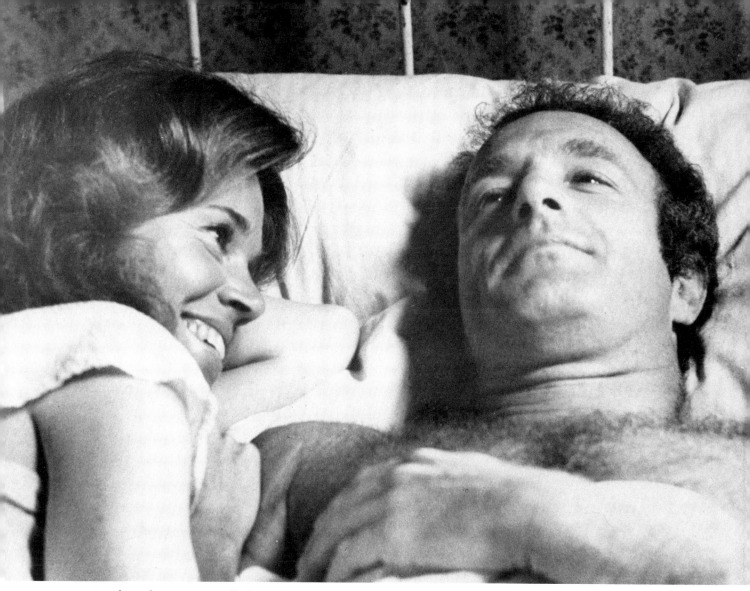

Fonda and Caan eventually become lovers and join to protect her land against corporate interests.

spinster (Fonda) and a good-natured World War II vet (Caan), who reluctantly pool their resources to battle a takeover by an expansionist landowner (Robards). The villain, meanwhile, has problems of his own: an oil company executive (George Grizzard) wants to plunder the cattle fields for crude. It is not difficult to guess what follows. Like every other so-called modern western, this one features a trusty old ranch hand (nicely played by Richard Farnsworth) who dies to symbolize the passing of the Old West. Like every old-fashioned western, *Horseman* slowly but surely sends its taciturn heroine into the macho hero's arms. Clark's climax, a plain old shootout, is surprising only because it is

capped by an optimistic denouement that contradicts everything that has come before.

Pakula seems incapable of visual sloppiness or vulgarity. He has also coaxed a performance from Fonda that is superior to her rather saintly appearances in *Julia* and *Coming Home.* Her face as weather-beaten as her dad's in *The Grapes of Wrath,* this beautiful woman manages to capture the essence of frontier toughness in the film's first half. When she finally melts for a man, Fonda's blushing radiance almost melts a movie that has long since congealed.

Stephen Farber, *New West:* Fonda etches still another brilliant characterization. This time

213

she's a fiercely independent frontierswoman who's wary of any human contact. She mistrusts everyone and she won't allow any emotional relationship to distract her from her overriding obsession with the land. Her pride is both commanding and maddening, and Fonda doesn't try to soften the character or make her lovable. She makes us think of those old photographs of Western matriarchs with leathery skin and the glint of steel in their eyes. There's an entire history of American tenacity in the rich character that Fonda creates.

Comes a Horseman is out of balance because Caan has nothing to learn from Fonda. He's a proud but gentle man who teaches the cold-hearted heroine how to love. In the later parts of the film Fonda recedes into the background as Caan takes the reins and tames her. Pakula's films often demonstrate a subtle but troubling sexual prejudice. He is fascinated by strong women but also seems somewhat frightened of them; he wants to put them in their place. In *The Sterile Cuckoo* the abrasive Liza Minnelli was finally rejected by the sensitive hero; in *Klute* Jane Fonda was rescued from degradation by supercop Donald Sutherland. *Comes a Horseman* reworks the same story: a strong, proud woman "realizes" that her salvation comes in submitting to an even stronger man. My objections to this solution are esthetic as well as political; the drama evaporates after the heroine melts.

Fonda and Caan square dance to celebrate their first cattle sale.

California Suite

Columbia, 1978. Directed by Herbert Ross. Produced by Ray Stark. Screenplay by Neil Simon, based on his play.
PRINCIPAL CAST (in alphabetical order): Alan Alda, Michael Caine, Bill Cosby, Jane Fonda, Walther Matthau, Elaine May, Richard Pryor, Maggie Smith.

IN THE WAKE OF three laudably serious films that restored her box-office stature and established her in many minds as the country's best actress, Jane Fonda undertook her second Neil Simon effort and first comedy since *Fun with Dick and Jane*. Actually, though *California Suite* was classified as a comedy, the quarter of the film that co-starred Fonda was on the dramatic side. Her role was an unrelentingly serious, hardened New Yorker; her lighter half was Alan Alda, an actor-activist who shares many of her views, especially on the subject of feminism and the ERA.

"I had never before known a man who called himself a feminist," she marveled. "We got along great." However, she took pains to explain that the role of Hannah was not one she identified with. Far from preferring East to West, city to beach, Fonda strongly prefers the California lifestyle to New York City life. Alda, on the other hand, feels more positive about big cities and the East Coast—he continues to live in New Jersey and commutes by plane to his work in Hollywood.

This assignment was short but an enjoyable change of pace for Jane, made in Los Angeles rather than on location. She got on especially well with Alda, Simon, and director Herbert Ross. And she didn't object to doing her first bit of cheesecake since *Barbarella*—a beach scene with Alda. Both wore swimsuits, in her case a purple bikini showing off a splendid figure, and in her shortened bob, she looked about a decade younger than her forty years.

She told inquiring reporters, "I've been doing ballet for twenty years or so. I try to spend an hour a day exercising hard [which she now does at her Jane Fonda's Workout]. The result is that I have a smaller waist than when I was around twenty."

The chemistry between Fonda and Alda prompted reports that they might work together again, and both campaigned together for the ERA. The snappy banter in their scenes together was a highlight of the uneven motion picture. Fonda remarked, "The dialogue is fast and sophisticated. It's the kind of quick repartee that harkens back to the bright, brittle screen comedies of the good old days. But there's more to it than that. Seriousness underlies it, giving people something to think about. It has depth. I wouldn't have done it if this were just a string of gags or slapstick." She had already determined that all her projects, even comedies, must have "something to say."

Director Ross tried to explain the point of the film: "It's about understanding the other person's weakness. In the case of Alan Alda and Jane Fonda they come to realize that one must let go. In the Maggie Smith–Michael Caine involvement, love wins out over mere sexuality. With Walter Matthau and Elaine May, the audience is presented with the fact that infidelity is not a deadly sin but simply a matter of human erring, as long as it doesn't become a habit. The point which is made about Richard Pryor and Bill Cosby's friendship is that good friends always transcend differences of opinion."

The movie was a glossy, well-received holiday package that made a fortune and enhanced the reputations of most of the actors involved, in particular Jane, Michael Caine—playing an un-

216

Jane Fonda shows off her splendid form in one of th[e] four Neil Simon stories comprising California Suite

CS-3

sensational homosexual, widely deemed his best-ever portrayal—and Maggie Smith, whose role as an Oscar loser became a real-life Oscar winner, her second win and her first in the supporting category.

Among all *California Suite*'s characters, Fonda's Hannah was perhaps the least likable. She explained why she chose to undertake her first unsympathetic role in a long time:

I'd just finished four pictures back to back, and felt I needed the challenge of a structured theatrical piece. Everyone knows that actors don't improvise Neil Simon. And if you're doing something that's much closer to you, something you're improvising, as we did a lot in *Coming Home*, it's not as challenging from an actor's point of view.

The role was demanding from another angle, too. I don't like the kind of woman I play in *California Suite* very much. She's a type I'm afraid people think I'm really like, so there's a tendency to put a distance between her and myself, and that's no good. It was so demanding it scared me to death, but I enjoyed doing it tremendously.

[Hannah] is a snob. She's uppity about California, for instance. She's the kind of person that George Wallace would describe as a pointy-headed East Coast intellectual who thinks that Californians have scrambled brains. Actually, I think anyone who lives in New York is kind of nuts.

I don't like the way she behaves. Probably wouldn't care for the people she hangs out with. I don't like bitches, and she's a bitch. Of course, she's acting that way to defend her vulnerabilities, but I don't agree with her choices.

REVIEWS:
Newsweek: There are those who can't resist Neil Simon and those—like this reviewer—who can. . . . In the most serious of the plotlets, Alda and Fonda are an estranged couple fighting over

On a California beach, Jane Fonda and Alan Alda discuss the custody of their teenage daughter.

Having come to an understanding, Fonda and Alda part, in an emotional scene.

the custody of their 17-year-old daughter. He's a laid-back Hollywood screen writer and she's a tough-as-nails *Newsweek* editor from New York, and the confrontation takes the form of East Coast vs. West Coast put-downs. Though Fonda and Alda are fascinating to watch and Simon frequently draws satirical blood, this particular game of cultural Ping Pong is beginning to seem a little provincial and passé.

Cue: Alan Alda and Jane Fonda (she's particularly good) perform with flair and feeling as a divorced couple waging a tug of war over their daughter; Maggie Smith steals the picture as an acid-tongued, vulnerable Oscar nominee, and

Michael Caine is memorable as her devoted homosexual husband. . . . An incredible lapse of taste and judgment occurs in the treatment of the bickering couples vacationing together. The blacks (Doctors Bill Cosby and Richard Pryor and wives Sheila Frazier and Gloria Gifford) are depicted as utter buffoons in a display of embarrassingly heavy-handed slapstick at total odds with the rest of the film.

Time: To call *California Suite* uneven doesn't begin to describe the movie's split personality. [It] is by turns silly and thoughtful, tedious and charming, broad and delicate. . . .

Jane Fonda and Alan Alda fare only fairly in

219

their sketch. She plays a tart-tongued *Newsweek* editor who has flown West to fight with her ex-husband over the custody of their daughter. After exchanging some worn New York vs. Los Angeles one-liners, far inferior to Woody Allen's in *Annie Hall*, Fonda and Alda get all bittersweet. The heroine's lacerating wit, it turns out, is but a mask for her insecurity. The superficial writing is not helped by Alda's unprepossessing screen presence, Ross' melodramatic use of close-ups or by a gratuitous beach scene that exists only to show off Fonda in a bikini.

Stephen Farber, *New West:* No holiday season would be complete without a new Neil Simon comedy. . . . Two of the stories contain some of Simon's sharpest writing. . . . Fonda's Hannah Warren is a tough, testy, snobbish *Newsweek* editor from New York, while ex-husband Bill is a model of laid-back California casualness. As a transplanted New Yorker himself, Simon can identify with both antagonists, and he gives each of them a strong voice. Although Hannah isn't easy to like, she comes alive as one of the most vivid characters that Simon has ever created. Of course, he's lucky to have Jane Fonda interpreting his lines. This amazing actress gives her third superb performance of 1978. She conveys the restless intelligence and the offputting arrogance of a New York journalist, and she also illuminates the fears that underlie Hannah's brittle, bitchy façade. This episode is uncharacteristic of Simon; it's scintillating, poignant and thoroughly compelling.

People: Neil Simon's vignettes of five couples at war in the Beverly Hills Hotel are intercut smoothly and delightfully. Two of the pieces are erratic. Walther Matthau has a funny face and manner but not enough funny lines when his wife, Elaine May, finds a hooker in his room. Bill Cosby and Richard Pryor engage in what was obviously intended as a scherzo, but which degenerates into sad slapstick. The *Suite*'s two *andante* movements, however, more than carry the movie. Tough New York writer Jane Fonda and laid-back California scenarist Alan Alda, a long-divorced pair, disagree painfully about their daughter's future. And Michael Caine plays a gay antique dealer married to over-the-hill actress Maggie Smith. Affecting and funny, these two couples make the movie *California Bittersweet*.

The China Syndrome

Columbia, 1979. Directed by James Bridges. Produced by Michael Douglas. Screenplay by Mike Gray, T. S. Cook, and James Bridges.
PRINCIPAL CAST: Jane Fonda, Jack Lemmon, Michael Douglas, Scott Brady, James Hampton, Peter Donat.

TV REPORTER KIMBERLY WELLS is on a routine assignment at a nuclear power plant, accompanied by photographer Richard Adams. While touring the plant with the PR man they witness an accident, which is swept under the rug by the utility company. Unbeknownst to anyone, Adams has done what he was told not to: filmed within the plant itself. His film is evidence that the accident was a warning of a potential disaster of unthinkable proportions. Adams and Wells argue whether to reveal the story. Her boss would just as soon see her continue reporting

Michael Douglas, Jack Lemmon, and Jane Fonda in a publicity still for The China Syndrome.

221

Director James Bridges talks to Jane Fonda on the set.

trivia items, but Adams insists that the news be made public, and Wells breaks her first major story. Once the news is leaked there is antagonism between the station's management on one side and its corporate parent and the nuclear plant on the other.

Jack Godell, in charge of the plant, becomes the central character for the rest of the movie. He has never before doubted that his plant is accident-proof, and he is reluctant to talk with Wells when she probes for further information. After much self-appraisal and checking and double-checking, he becomes convinced that the plant is unsafe. He moves to deliver the pertinent information to Wells, to publicly dissemi-

nate the truth. His assistant, carrying the vital evidence in his car, is pursued by company goons who drive him off the road; he is nearly killed in the "accident," and the evidence disappears.

Godell himself is pursued on his way to a showdown at the plant, where he has invited Wells to meet him. He forcibly takes over the control room, allowing no one inside but the TV reporter. The truth is made public, but a SWAT team bursts into the control room and murders Godell with a shower of gunfire. The plant's management and PR man try to pass off Godell's revelations as the rantings and ravings of an overworked, mentally ill executive, but Wells fi-

222

nally extracts the credibility of Godell's mission from his shaken co-workers and shares it with TV viewers.

The China Syndrome was Fonda's biggest hit yet, a movie whose stunning world impact was due not only to its timely subject but also to the uncanny coincidence of the historic accident at Three Mile Island, which made international headlines and made nuclear energy the number-one topic of conversation for a while. Also aiding the film's success was its suspenseful and thrilling plot, its allusion to the real-life murder of Karen Silkwood, a massive publicity campaign involving its three stars, and the fact that Jane Fonda had never been more attractive.

Fonda's makeup artist, Bernadine, the first black female in the union, says, "Jane's a perfectionist. She always wants to break down the character, way before filming. We discuss how she should look, and she'll tell me, right down to the last hairpin."

After failing to obtain screen rights to the Karen Silkwood story, Fonda assumed Richard Dreyfuss's role in *Power* (the original title), which was Michael Douglas's first production since *One Flew over the Cuckoo's Nest*. Robert Scheer's series of articles in the *Los Angeles Times* about the grooming of TV newswomen prompted her to gain firsthand information about her character by covering news stories and doing extensive legwork with Los Angeles newswomen Connie Chung, Heidi Shulman, Robin Groth, Kelly Lange, and Jackie King. She

TV soundman Daniel Valdez, power-company public-relations man James Hampton, and reporter Jane Fonda are startled by cameraman Michael Douglas's insistence on telling the truth.

observed, "Feature reporting in the field is very hard work. Often, the story you've been sent out on just isn't there or isn't true. And it's pretty thin stuff to begin with. Once we went out to cover a fashion show because Betty Ford was supposed to attend. No Betty Ford; no story."

Jane explained her acting philosophy: "You always have to find something of yourself in whatever character you play, or you cannot act it. When Kimberly wants to pursue her story and her boss says, 'Don't worry your pretty head about all that,' I understood. It's hard for a pretty woman to be accepted on a level beyond or in contradiction to the stereotyped image of prettiness. Also, at certain points in my life I've had to choose between being what I considered to be socially responsible or guarantee that I am going to have a career, and like Kimberly, I chose to jeopardize a career."

Some of the initial press reaction to *The China Syndrome* was critical, pointing out the three stars' anti-nuclear-power bias. Nuclear-energy companies protested that the film's premise was an impossible fiction, and there was lobbying against the movie as companies with nuclear interests attempted to place articles offering a pro-nuclear point of view. General Electric withdrew its sponsorship of a program featuring a Barbara Walters interview of the actress, even though in the interview Fonda hardly touched upon her latest film.

Then came Harrisburg. The lines at the cinemas lengthened. Columbia Pictures ceased advertising the picture; it was thought best to keep a low profile regarding the real-life accident, and anyway, the incident had generated more than enough publicity for the film. Coincidentally, one of the movie's lines referred to the possibility of rendering uninhabitable "an area the size of Pennsylvania."

Three Mile Island benefited not only the picture, but Jane Fonda's credibility. Cover stories in *Time* and *Newsweek* prominently tied *The China Syndrome* in with the whole nuclear issue, and of course, the actress shortly waged a national campaign against nuclear power plants. One *Newsweek* letter to the editor half-jested,

I read with interest George F. Will's attack on Jane Fonda's film *The China Syndrome*, which included an accusation that Fonda has invented nuclear fantasies about melting cores in the interest of satisfying her own greed. However, Will had the misfortune of having his piece see print during the same week that the Harrisburg incident reared its ugly head. We Americans are notoriously thickheaded, but must even the journalists of this country have to relearn the hard lesson that Jane Fonda is usually right?
Robert E. Rodi
Oak Brook, Illinois.

The China Syndrome yielded Jane's fifth Oscar nomination, her third in a row.

REVIEWS:

Circus: Jane Fonda, looking stunning, plays Kimberly Wells, a television newswoman who visits a nuclear power plant and witnesses Jack Lemmon, the plant foreman, with a near-disaster on his hands. . . . The suspense here makes *Invasion of the Body Snatchers* look like a picnic. Will the atomic plant blow up? Will Jane and Michael (Douglas) save the day? The danger is very real—it could happen in a number of major cities—though the energy industry has been lobbying against the film. Lemmon finally locks himself in the control room and tries to tell the world. The ending is upbeat but what goes before it won't leave you feeling too reassured. The chairman of the utility and his minions are painted as black-hearted villains willing to kill to protect their profits and the TV executives are afraid to run the story. Like *Network*, this one looks at the responsibility of the press and finds it wanting.

Time: It is hard to recall a movie of recent years as absorbing or as much fun as *The China Syndrome*. . . . The credit belongs in part to director Bridges for his sure handling of the action and in part to a script that makes us really care for Fonda and Lemmon. It seems almost superfluous to praise Fonda anew but she is truly at the peak of her talent these days. Nobody has done a better characterization of the vacuity of

225

Douglas and Fonda think they're on to a gigantic story of nuclear danger and a coverup of the facts.

the TV news "personality"—the little moments of make-up-mirror vanity snatched against deadline pressure, the falseness of on-camera performances that must never really look like performances, the psychological confusions of pretending to be a real reporter when you know you've been hired because you've got good bones. Lemmon, through the sheer integrity of his playing—no cute stuff, no obvious plays for sympathy—is outstanding as an essentially lonely man who has built his life around his dials and gauges and then learns that they have been programmed from the start to deceive him.

Cue: The rare combination of an urgent message and vigorous entertainment has been smashingly realized in *The China Syndrome*, a sizzling, nerve-shattering thriller about individ-

ual conscience and the danger of nuclear accident. . . . Jane Fonda is so splendidly dynamic and realistic as ambitious Los Angeles reporter Kimberly Wells that she could replace anyone on the tube—except that she'd be too good for the job. . . . Using authentic-looking sets, director James Bridges packs the film with detail about both the nuclear and broadcasting operations and keeps the story crackling at a feverish pace reminiscent of *Z*. *The China Syndrome*, which also sparkles with true-to-life dialogue, solid supporting performances and excellent photography and editing, is gripping from start to finish.

Richard Grenier, *Cosmopolitan: The China Syndrome* is a taut, frightening, thrillingly effective tract against nuclear power, eerily anticipat-

Conscience at war with job security—an angry confrontation between Fonda and Douglas.

Jane Fonda interviews an important witness, Jack Lemmon, as Michael Douglas watches.

ing some of the terrifying events in Harrisburg. The title refers to what professionals call a "melt down"—a catastrophic interruption of a plant's cooling system which theoretically could cause the installation to sink all the way through to China. . . . Fonda and Douglas play a kind of anti-atomic Woodward-Bernstein and Lemmon a conscience-stricken whistle-blower. En route to its stunning conclusion the plot is laced with attempted murder and finally, a genuine homicide in the service of a cover-up (shades of the Karen Silkwood case). . . . Jane Fonda is absolutely electric as the ambitious reporter, while Jack Lemmon, in his best role in years, captures the full anguish of the tormented technician.

Norma McLain Stoop, *After Dark: The China Syndrome* is a terrifically exciting, brilliantly directed film that sweats suspense. The tense screenplay has you holding on to your seatbelts at all times. This is a story of consciences and kings: the consciences of reliable men and women and the tough pragmatism of kings of industry. . . . Jane Fonda sends off sparks as a soft-news TV gal who gets and fights to keep a hard-news story about the cover-up of an "accident" at the nuclear plant and, in the process, finds out the hard facts about hard news. She's wonderful. . . . Terrifying as it is, this film is much more than a thriller. *The China Syndrome* is a film to see and to recommend to your friends. It's a film full of urgency that cannot be dismissed. Power is what *The China Syndrome* is all about.

Charles Champlin, *Los Angeles Times:* Jane Fonda is a bubbly TV newsperson covering animal birthdays at the zoo and yearning to taste

the hard stuff. . . . There are two brief but very effective car sequences. Daniel Valdez as an aide to Douglas and then Lemmon himself are the more startled and scared because the pursuits seem so unthinkable, and for the viewers the resulting chases are correspondingly scarier. . . . Some laughable demonstrations dramatize the puniness of the opposition to the expansion of nuclear power. The movie is, obviously, rather a different matter. General Electric, which equips nuclear plants, is reported to have canceled its sponsorship of a Barbara Walters–Jane Fonda interview because of Ms. Fonda's participation in *The China Syndrome*. Fonda is reported to have said, "What are they afraid of? It's only a movie"—a remark whose mocking irony will presumably not be lost on Schenectady (GE headquarters). . . . Fonda's role is, despite some high-tension scenes at the end, less interior than her evolving military wife in *Coming Home*. Her change here from self-centered career girl to concerned fighter is an inevitable result of external events. But she is, as always, commanding and convincing at both ends of the character.

In the film's moving climax, an angry and stunned Fonda tells the TV audience what has happened.

The Electric Horseman

Columbia-Universal, 1979. Directed by Sydney Pollack. Produced by Ray Stark. Screenplay by Robert Garland, from a screen story by Garland and Paul Gaer, based on a story by Shelly Burton. PRINCIPAL CAST: Robert Redford, Jane Fonda, Valerie Perrine, Willie Nelson, John Saxon, Let's Merge (horse).

ACCORDING TO ONE WAG, the story of *The Electric Horseman* is boy meets horse, boy gets horse, boy meets girl along the way, girl gets boy, boy loses horse on purpose, girl gets scoop. It wasn't a typical love story, nor could it be, for its stars were Robert Redford, the number-one box-office actor, and Jane Fonda, the number-one box-office actress. Redford's films were mostly pure entertainment, whereas Fonda's have long been at least partial mirrors of her own beliefs; thus,

Jane Fonda in another role as a TV news reporter.

Fonda attempts to fol. Robert Redford across wilderness wearing Redford puts it, "b from Bloomingbira

Electric was an amalgam of their two personalities. Advertised as a love story with an ecological twist, *Electric*'s romance was minimal and didn't occur until the end. After their passion had spent itself in a single night, the two protagonists went their separate ways, Redford casually moving on and Fonda returning to her well-paid, high-pressured job as a TV newswoman, a more sophisticated version of her *China Syndrome* role.

Sonny Steele is a jaded cowboy and rodeo champ who sells breakfast cereal for a living and drinks for a hobby. He is separated from his wife, Carlotta, played as a cameo by sometime sex symbol Valerie Perrine. (Willie Nelson makes his movie debut as a hanger-on.) Steele is brought to Las Vegas to participate in the convention of the company that owns the breakfast cereal. He gets to know the beautiful horse that is the conglomerate's corporate logo and is being drugged and chemically treated for esthetic reasons and to make it more docile beneath the bright showroom lights.

Steele is shaken out of his lethargy when, on the spur of the moment—during a stage number studded with jiggling chorus girls—he kidnaps the horse so he can set it free in the wilderness, where it may return to a natural, unspoiled way of life, the kind of life Sonny himself now yearns for. In the meantime, Jane Fonda as Hallie Martin, an ambitious TV newswoman, takes up his scent and tracks him down in the Utah desert. She becomes involved with the electric horseman and comes to laud his noble gesture, aiding him in his escape from the pursuing authorities.

There are plenty of lines about New York, women, horses, nature, and personal identity, as the couple wend their way through awe-inspiring scenery. Finally they kiss, spend a night of romance, and deliver the prize horse to freedom at an unspecified site. Public opinion has sided with Steele against the conglomerate, and after Hallie and Sonny part, she reports her story on national TV, turning the horseman into a folk hero.

Nature and ecology have long been close to the hearts of both Fonda and Redford, and *The*

Electric Horseman mirrors this, as well as anticorporate feeling. Some critics found the movie's corporate bad guys too stereotypical, but the message was discreet. So was the feminism in Fonda's role: After she was slapped by Steele, she slapped back vigorously and called him a son of a bitch. The ending didn't find Martin falling into love and marriage; instead, she maintained her own identity and lifestyle.

The Electric Horseman was a co-production of Redford's Wildwood company, and he reportedly received a three-million-dollar salary, as well as a healthy percentage. By contrast, Fonda received a mere one million dollars which still made her one of the highest-paid actresses in the world. Much was made of the stellar salaries, and during location shooting in Utah and Nevada it was announced that Jane would get two million dollars for her next vehicle, the biggest fee ever paid an American actress (Streisand and Taylor made more on *A Star Is Born* and *Cleopatra*, respectively, thanks to percentage deals).

Though neither star had to do much in the way of acting (many critics seemed disenchanted by Fonda's taking another role so similar to Kimberly Wells), filming didn't go smoothly. A series of storms interrupted shooting in Saint George, Utah (Redford's home state—as a state taxpayer he benefited by having the movie made there), for several weeks. One simple kissing scene necessitated forty-eight takes. That meant poor Jane had to kiss Robert Redford forty-eight times, between nine A.M. on a Tuesday and six P.M. the next day. To cover the kiss from every angle more than seventy-five hundred feet of film was shot, all for a sequence lasting twenty seconds in the movie. Their kiss cost an estimated $280,000, and the cost accountant complained, "It would have been cheaper if Redford had kissed the horse."

Came time for the ad campaign, it was decided to deemphasize the word *Horseman* in the title, which might give audiences the idea the film was a western (*Comes a Horseman* had not fared well financially). The love story and the battle-of-the-sexes angle were played up. The photo in the ads, over which was emblazoned the word *Electric*, featured a rear view of Red-

Robert Redford, a champion rodeo rider, has stolen a million-dollar horse, and Jane Fonda has followed him Here, he awakens her after their first night in the des

ford in denim holding an upside-down Fonda. It looked as if they were scrapping or as if Redford were about to toss Fonda into a pool. Actually, the photo was a candid, taken while Redford and Fonda were horsing around during a break.

During its first week of release, *Electric* became the top-grossing film in the country, exhibiting surprising staying power during the following months, primarily because of the appeal of its two legendary stars.

REVIEWS:

Lawrence O'Toole, *McLean's:* Robert Redford: God, but he's gaudy. His teeth seem forged from some Nordic myth, his hair spun by those sisters of Fate, The Three Norns, on a par-

ticularly desperate lonely night to amuse themselves. Even the several moles on the right side of his face are dramatically decorative. And he obviously tears into his Wheaties at sunrise. One's first response to Redford is: grossly unfair. . . . Put him in a satin cowboy shirt of a purplish hue—a shirt that lights up, already—and you're not talking just turkey, you're talking unicorn or something. Put Jane Fonda in leather pants and hitch her heart to his in the stunning, wide-open spaces of Utah, have them change into denim, and it's practically pornographic. They're the Marlboro Couple.

A sharp journalist—Fonda, Ms. Journalism herself—pursues him for his story as he treks across the great divide. . . . She discovers there is more than one stallion and, lucky girl, gets

Relations between Fonda and Redford have been chilly. Now they're beginning to warm up.

A tender moment as Jane Fonda touches one of Robert Redfor's many scars—mementos of rodeo injuries.

considerably more than she bargained for. . . . "You're just walking around to save funeral expenses," his ex-wife, Valerie Perrine, tells him, and there is that sense of don't-care-nohow, give-me-another-shot-of-that-juice in Redford's performance. But Fonda's too coiled and tight; she has a fuzzy grip on a fuzzy character. There's no tension in the chase, no witty banter between the two—just the great outdoors and denim. Proving even the Marlboro Couple needs help.

Merrill Shindler, *Los Angeles:* Like Tolkien's *Lord of the Rings,* Sydney Pollack's *The Electric Horseman* is a quest in reverse. Frodo's purpose was to carry the One Ring of Power back to its source at Mount Doom and thereby free us all.

Robert Redford, as Sonny Steele, has a far simpler purpose. He wants to release a Triple Crown–winning stallion named Rising Star in a canyon where no one will find him ever again. By doing so, Sonny will not only free one fine horse, he'll also give a brief respite to that old cowboy spirit, the spirit that magazines like *Esquire* keep telling us lives on only in Tony Lama boots and shrink-to-fit Levi's.

The film turns into a decent but fairly regulation chase film. Reporter Jane Fonda, apparently on assignment in Las Vegas after her ambiguous coverage of events in *The China Syndrome,* goes chasing after Sonny to find out the real poop on why he took the horse—and to supply film at eleven, as they say in the trade. Against the backdrop of the glorious Utah Rockies, Fonda and Redford spend the rest of the film playing out a westernized version of Lina Wertmuller's *Swept Away,* swapping witty repartee and snappy patter, going to bed, getting into misunderstandings and, in time, letting the horse go.

Time: Her name is Hallie Martin. She is played by Jane Fonda. She is a TV newswoman, very chic and ambitious for a big story, though looking for it in an unlikely place, the conglomerate's annual meeting at Caesars Palace in Las Vegas. . . . Boy gets horse. Girl gets story (and also ceases to be merely a pesky observer and becomes an impassioned participant in Sonny's adventure). The populace learns the truth about the evil capitalists and rallies to the side of the beleaguered rebels. Why, boy and girl even get each other, if briefly.

Yet rarely in recent years has this basic tale been told in such an agreeably inventive way. . . . Due credit to Fonda: here, in direct contrast to the development of a similar character in *The China Syndrome,* she moves from knowledgeability to vulnerability, and does it with the same winning grace. . . . It's obvious both stars saw this film as a vehicle to advocate causes they care about, but they are good-natured about it. . . . A romantic intensity that Fonda and Redford might have generated is lost as a result. . . . Still, there is not a more cheerful or engaging movie around these days. One can't

Fonda and Redford head for Utah, where they plan to release the horse in the wild.

help coming out of it in smiling good temper, having spent a fine time with nice but catchily eccentric people.

Newsweek: Will we ever see Jane Fonda and Robert Redford playing unvirtuous people, people on the wrong side of the great issues, scurvy meanies, wrongos instead of rightos? Don't bet on it. That's too bad, because we need Lady MacBeths as well as Cordelias, Iagos as well as Othellos, and you'd think that high-voltage actors like Fonda and Redford would want to transmit both the negative and positive electricity in human beings. Since these stars are celebrated mavericks, supposedly resistant to movie-biz stereotyping, it's interesting that they seem to see themselves as behavioral models, icons of righteousness pointing the way toward proper conduct in a corrupting world. Righteousness blends with their grace and beauty: you don't have their grace and beauty but you certainly can be righteous, so if you'll only agree with them on whatever it is—the Vietnam war, nuclear energy, the environment—you too can have the golden flair and ethical sexiness of Fonda and Redford. In *The Electric Horseman* they're at their most golden, ethical and sexy. . . . In their love scenes they actually make you believe that pure virtue is the strongest of aphrodisiacs.

238

Andrew Sarris, *Village Voice:* Redford and Fonda are actually involved in a weird sort of Bazinian epiphany by traversing the wide open spaces of Utah itself. Fonda, both on-screen and off, must move on, of course, but Redford will stay in this idyllic wilderness of his liberal imagination. Their on-screen one-night stand takes on a poignant quality in light of their long struggle for stardom. Their youth is gone but they are still beautiful, and there is something more to them off the screen, something to which their screen images refer without ever explicitly identifying that "something's" precise nature. For all their desperate quest for reality and authenticity, they remind me of a time when I still believed in movie stars, and thus I treasure *The Electric Horseman* for the reminder.

Stephen Farber, *New West.* If we resist the movie at first it may be because we can't help feeling wary of a $12.5 million Hollywood extravaganza that is conceived as an attack on materialism and a paean to the simple life. We never do surrender wholeheartedly, but at least the anti-materialistic message isn't pushed too strenuously.

Ten years ago Sydney Pollack directed *They Shoot Horses, Don't They?*, a movie that summed up the cynicism of the '60s as it chronicled the death of the American dream. Now, at the end of another decade . . . Pollack has made a movie that reaffirms all the American ideals that *They Shoot Horses* repudiated. This new film says that one person can defy the corporate conglomerates; it says that America is still a land of possibility. At one point Redford and Fonda even join in singing a verse of "America the Beautiful." . . . In its own way *Electric* is as irresistible a piece of Americana as *Stagecoach* or *High Noon.*

Playgirl: The stolen horse is a hot news item to ace TV reporter Jane Fonda, so when Redford takes off she follows with the corporate baddies behind her. So far *Electric Horseman* has been fun (despite its transparent metaphors for corruption), but the moment the chase begins the picture goes down the tubes. Even with its load of energy-sapping drugs the horse outruns an army of car and motorcycle-mounted police. And, most cynically of all, the script wants us to believe that the country folks who help Redford and Fonda are essentially more noble than the city folks who chase them. Damn, I kept thinking, ain't them country ways sweet! Maybe so, but this here's one city boy who ain't recommendin' that other city folks indulge their self-hatred by paying to see *Electric Horseman.*

Nine to Five

20th Century-Fox, 1980. Directed by Colin Higgins. Produced by Bruce Gilbert. Screenplay by Colin Higgins and Patricia Resnick; story by Patricia Resnick.
PRINCIPAL CAST: *Jane Fonda, Lily Tomlin, Dolly Parton, Dabney Coleman, Elizabeth Wilson, and Sterling Hayden.*

"JANE IS VERY INTENSE. She's a strong presence in a movie—I felt that when we started. I did a picture years ago called *A Child Is Waiting* with Judy Garland, and she is the only other person in whom I felt all that centered concentration. Being on screen with Garland, she had this glow, an intense and powerful thing. Jane has it, too."

The words came from veteran actress Elizabeth Wilson, who co-starred with Fonda in her first 1980s film, *Nine to Five.* The hit comedy about three secretaries—with social ramifica-

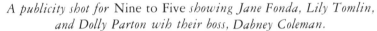

A publicity shot for Nine to Five *showing Jane Fonda, Lily Tomlin, and Dolly Parton wih their boss, Dabney Coleman.*

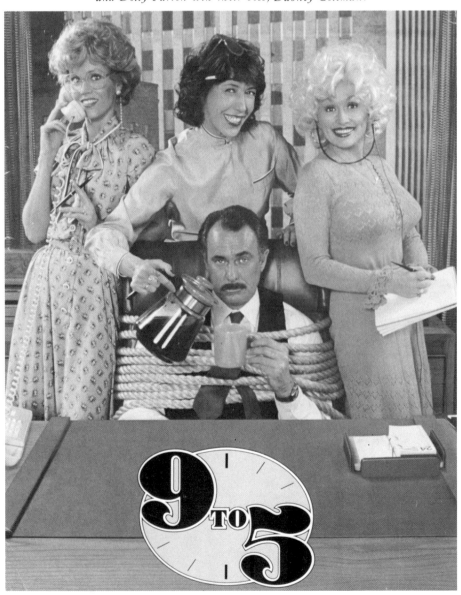

240

Parton, Tomlin, and Fonda commiserate over drinks, just before they come up with madcap schemes to get even with their male-chauvinist boss.

tions, of course—starred the winning team of Jane, Lily Tomlin and newcomer (to films) Dolly Parton. It was the fourth production involving IPC Films, Jane's production company.

Once a secretary herself, Fonda had long been interested in the plight and rights of secretaries, among other working women. She and partner Bruce Gilbert had responded favorably to a story by a woman writer about secretaries who take revenge on a chauvinistic male boss. Then came writer-director Colin Higgins, an Australian-American who had written the cult classic *Harold and Maude* and had written and directed the comedy hits *Silver Streak* and *Foul Play*.

From the beginning, *Nine to Five* was planned as a tripartite vehicle for Jane, feminist Lily Tomlin, and singer Dolly Parton, who wrote the title song.

In between hilarious predicaments, the three principals discover that the business world, and the secretarial world in particular, is unfair, if not exactly a drudge. At Higgins's insistence, the ending is optimistic. "For me," he explained, "it's a totally optimistic universe. At the darkest hour, the clouds open up and everything is set right again. *Love,*" he added, "is actually the one word I think of in trying to sum up all three ladies. Working with Jane, particularly during the long, hard months of getting the script into shape, I found her to be wonderfully supportive and helpful. She is warm and witty and a lot of fun to be around."

Fonda played a fortyish character named Judy Bernly, described as a recently divorced housewife taking the first job of her "male-defined life." Though the Tomlin and Parton characters were equal in importance, the movie's audience saw things from Judy's point of view. Lily Tomlin played Violet Newstead, top woman on the secretarial floor. (Tomlin's previously completed starring picture *The Incredible Shrinking Woman* was held back for release until after *Nine to Five,* so the latter's success might rub off on the former.) Violet's problem was that despite her intelligence and ability, she never got a promotion. The men she trained kept passing over her, for women weren't considered for major positions.

Dolly Parton essayed a big-hearted (but not dumb, as she made very clear) southern executive secretary named Doralee Rhodes, on whom boss Dabney Coleman cast a constantly lecherous eye. Sterling Hayden played Consolidated bigwig Mr. Tinsworthy, and Elizabeth Wilson took on the thankless role of Roz, an office Benedict Arnold who ratted on "the girls" to the boss.

In her thirty-third film, Jane Fonda made another effort to lose herself in a character and to not suffuse Judy Bernly with her own strong personality. Again, she started with Judy's look, the outer self that reflects what's inside a character. After a few conferences with costume designer Ann Roth, Jane opted for a conservative, too-fem wardrobe. Explained Roth, "The first outfit Jane wears is unsuited to office life—especially the hat. She wears a certain uniform which was determined when she was a child going out with her mother—they're nice-girl clothes, and there are rules about these things." Example: the *de rigueur* navy-blue bag with navy-blue shoes.

Jane wore an "uptight" wig, eyeglasses with little chains attached, and "a prim but frilly" wardrobe to develop the role. She noted, "I went about seeking out women who had entered the job market late in life because they were recently widowed or divorced. . . . One thing that they all told me was how they arrived overdressed on the first day. How they felt out of

Elizabeth Wilson, the administrative assistant to a corporate executive, has been spying on her co-workers.

Fonda, Tomlin, and Parton begin making waves in the typing pool.

place. These women faced tremendous psychological difficulties, and they feared entering a situation where all the other women were professionals who had been there much of their lives."

Nine to Five could have been a drama, perhaps even a thriller, for it mirrored many sobering, unjust truths. But Fonda had shied away from heavyhanded, possibly alienating messages, and she and Bruce Gilbert decided on comedy as the medium for their entertaining message:

"We visited the headquarters of the National Association of Office Workers in Cleveland," said Gilbert of the movie's research. "At a certain point, we asked the women if they had ever fantasized about getting even with their bosses. That was like opening a floodgate. Suddenly, the most bizarre and funny stories started coming out, and it certainly reinforced our decision to do the film as a comedy."

Patricia Resnick had researched the original story by going undercover at a large insurance-brokerage firm and an employment agency, and Jane had become involved with activities on behalf of a Los Angeles secretaries' group. The movie credits included the producers' grateful acknowledgement of "the help and encouragement of working women, the National Association of Office Workers, in the making of this film."

This is a good place to mention more about Bruce Gilbert, Jane's collaborator in three of her top films, for he will definitely play an increasingly large role in her future career. Gilbert declared, "I never started out wanting to produce movies. I was interested in how to present information, to help people learn, to change attitudes. I was training to become a developmental psychologist, not a Hollywood movie producer.

243

Tomlin, Parton, and Fonda are entertaining each other with fantasies of revenge.

I'm still interested in ideas, information, and how to communicate them. It's just that the scale of the audience has changed. Actually, there is more to it than that.

"On a feature film I have to help figure out how to take my abstract research—whether it's about Vietnam vets, nuclear power plants, office life, or whatever—and infuse it with a dramatic structure and interesting characters. That's the hardest part. It takes so long to develop a movie, it just has to be something to be proud of in the end. Some people want to make movies for the money, but I can't understand that. There are just too many headaches and stumbling blocks along the way for that to be the basic motivating force."

Jane offered, "I wouldn't have gotten into production if not for Bruce. In order to produce movies, you have to be an administrator. You have to know how to negotiate. You have to understand money and business. Those are not my strengths, but they are Bruce's. We share a similar commercial sense, have the same tastes, and want to make the same kind of movies. And Bruce is also in charge of the research we do for our projects. He's extraordinarily good at that."

Said Gilbert, "Either Jane or I will come up with a subject that's interesting to both of us. Everyone else seems to think that's backward, but we decide what we want to say first and *then* develop the story. I'll usually do some research and start compiling background, and then Jane and I will throw ideas back and forth until we have a sort of spine for the story. Then we look for a writer whom we feel is best suited for the material.

245

Jane Fonda is trying to figure out the vagaries of a new machine.

"While researching *Nine to Five* we spoke to many women and learned a great deal about the undercurrents of what goes on in big offices. We asked the women to tell us about their jobs and their complaints, and we found again and again that the major problem was in the area of self-respect. They feel that you can run an office without bosses, but not without secretaries. They also feel that there's no real recognition of that fact."

Fonda found that "one of the stereotypes I had heard about secretaries was not true. I'd heard that these women didn't like their work, that they would be doing something else if they could. But without exception, the women I spoke to liked their work. They had become independent and liked that, too. And they all recognized the importance of what they do. It *is* important work. It's skilled work. The problem isn't with the job so much as how management treats their secretaries, showing a lack of respect that reflects itself in wages, lack of promotion, and the menial tasks they're asked to do.

"I wanted to show through my character a woman who comes to work with the fear and trepidation of someone new to the office and who comes to take pride in what she's learned. She's a bit of a klutz in the beginning, but she likes the fact that she learns to master all the office equipment and that she can then teach someone else all the things she's learned. She's good at what she does, and she knows it."

Nine to Five was shot partly on Stage 6 at 20th Century-Fox, where a million dollars was spent to construct an appropriately up-to-date office set. It was the same stage used for the 1957 office comedy *Desk Set*, with Katharine Hepburn, Spencer Tracy, Joan Blondell, and Dina Merrill; the three women played co-workers in a research center. Today, Jane has offices at Fox—

Fonda appears wide eyed as Coleman explains office procedures.

perhaps the most pro-actress studio in Hollywood—and she reportedly has various Fox projects in the offing, including more female-buddy films. "I've always been a fan of the great movies of the forties that had three female stars. I think it's time to do movies like that again."

Recalling the past, Fonda mused on future directions: "I spent almost twenty years as an actress before I managed to take some control over my work. Very frankly, I didn't often enjoy my work as an actress very much. There would always be particular scenes in some movies that I would remember fondly, and of course there were *They Shoot Horses, Don't They?* and *Klute.* But there was no real expression of myself, and I probably didn't have too much to express at the beginning anyway. I mean, if I had the opportunity, I don't know what I would have wanted to say. I guess, like most actresses, I was just interested in a good part.

"But the idea of giving up acting now is inconceivable to me. And Bruce is largely responsible for helping to effect this major change of attitude. My friends helped persuade me that there was value in acting and, particularly, that I could contribute through my filmwork. That's when I decided not to be so passive any more, and I began to take an active involvement in the projects I worked on. Now I make movies about subjects that interest me.

"*The China Syndrome* is actually about work. There's very little in it that doesn't have to do with work. And *Nine to Five* is of course about work. Most of us spend a major portion of our waking hours at work, and we're not particularly conscious about it. It determines everything about our lives."

On IPC's future, Jane stated, "There are just certain stories that are better suited for television, and besides, I am acutely aware that a

Fonda responds to something her supervisor, Tomlin, has said.

whole lot of people in this country don't go to movies. They can't afford it or don't have time. I grew up with this sort of elitist attitude about television, and I'd like to try to reverse that. I want to do both. Bruce and I are interested in communicating, and we feel very strongly about developing a whole television arm.

"There are absolutely brilliant actresses in this country whom I would love our company to produce things for. There's room for all of us. I don't see myself stopping my work as an actress as I get older." But she added, "I don't think that I have the particular skills that make for a great director. I'm too emotional. I'm sort of lazy, which may surprise people. But I like the fact that someone else is ultimately responsible. Film is a director's medium, and I like to work in a collaborative situation, but when the day is over I like to go home and forget about it. That's hard for a director to do."

The ever-busy top female box-office star in the world feels, "It's all tremendously gratifying.

It's wonderful when audiences or exhibitors or your peers tell you that you're doing a good job. But it's dangerous if you take it all too seriously. When you're hungry you allow yourself to take great leaps of faith, but when you start taking yourself too seriously, then you can lose that courage and start playing it safe. Don't ever start playing it safe."

As for Jane Fonda, private citizen, she concluded, "I don't attract attention to myself. I find that I can travel by myself. I can walk through public places and people may recognize me, but they don't particularly bother me. A lot of times I think that celebrities attract attention to themselves and sort of ask for trouble because of the way they dress and because of their entourage and the limos and all that. But if you behave like a normal person, people will respect that.

"I think that people perceive me as somebody who is feisty, and someone who commits wholeheartedly. Even though the characters I play aren't all feisty—and Judy Bernly certainly

The three rebellious employees begin to put their plan into action.

Parton, Fonda, and Tomlin attempting their getaway.

isn't—there's still a sense that I commit myself totally to the part. I think it goes along with a general perception of me as a person."

REVIEWS:

David Ansen, *Newsweek*: Jane Fonda. Lily Tomlin. Dolly Parton. If Oscars were given for the casting coup of the year, *Nine to Five* would win hands down. Demographically speaking, those three names constitute a star-studded net from which no prospective movie-goer can be expected to escape. And since the three portray secretaries who literally take arms against their ogre of a boss, the comedy should prove irresistible to every working woman in America. . . .

Fonda is the wide-eyed, newly divorced newcomer to the office jungle. Tomlin is the super-efficient veteran who keeps getting passed up for promotion. Parton is the warmhearted sexpot. . . . The three become pals and, while relaxing at home over a joint, share their pot-inspired fantasies of murdering their nemesis (Dabney Coleman). When Lily mistakenly puts rat poison in the boss' coffee, their fantasies begin to come true. Eventually they find themselves kidnapping the ogre, blackmailing him for embezzlement and instituting office reforms (day-care services, job-sharing, flexible hours), while maintaining the illusion that the boss is still at his desk.

Tomlin steals all available scenes with a deadpan delivery that puts a surreal spin on her commonsensical character. "I'm no fool," she says during the rat-poison episode. "I've killed the boss. You think they're not going to fire me for a thing like that?" Tomlin also gets the best fantasy—a Disneyesque cartoon in which she appears dressed like Snow White, dispensing death with a magic wand. . . . Fonda has the least appealing role, playing straight woman to her antic cohorts.

Nancy Scott, *San Francisco Chronicle*: Jane Fonda swivels the shotgun. She takes aim. Bam!

There goes the VDT. Bam! There go the IBM, the Rolodex, the push-button phone, the files, the glass doors. And bam! There goes the boss.

Whoopee! Hurray! I wish this were a recording; paper is too quiet, and I do not feel quiet about *Nine to Five,* a grand farce I enjoyed so much that making intelligent critical noises is about as much fun as whispering at a ballgame. . . . Not only feminists are likely to enjoy this movie, though it . . . is sometimes close to being a preachment. . . . And the final scenes are too close to a petition of demands from beleaguered office workers.

Fonda's fantasy turns the great impersonal office into a metaphorical swamp and transforms the boss into a man on the run, pursued by bloodhounds. Each fantasy is neatly suited to the woman, to her character, her anger, her predicament. Fonda's is the richest in the way it uses the place of work and the tools of work, the way it reverses authority, putting Fonda behind the boss' desk with a brash Aussie hat on her head and a shotgun in her hands. Fonda is so prissy, so fussy and so frightened that I forgot she was Fonda.

The heroes of farcical comedies like *Nine to Five* are traditionally foolish, likeable, put-upon characters, and they act for every one of us who has ever suffered working a machine or dealing with authority. And they are traditionally men. I think this is the first time I have seen women who were allowed to be heroes *and* foolish. It's wonderful.

Gerald Nachman, *San Francisco Examiner*: This comedy is a sort of *Norma Rae* for clerical workers. . . . Imagine reading the *National Lampoon* with an E.R.A. flyer stuck in every third page. . . . Jane Fonda is never less than wonderful in a new and unlikely timid guise, all prim blouses, sweet scarves and big round glasses.

One of the best things about *Nine to Five* is how it conveys the humdrum feel of a big cold inhuman company, rows of women typing, putting people on hold and copying reports on huge Xeroxes that eat secretaries alive. What spoils this reality is that all the men are straw sexists. . . . The boss not only looks and acts like G.

Gordon Liddy, at one point he even twirls his moustache. . . . Surprisingly, the silly stuff is more delicately handled than the feminism.

Tomlin is crisp and zippy and gives the movie its satiric soul. While Tomlin's on screen, God's in Her heaven. Fonda, in a more subdued way, is funnier than she's ever been (also sexier—oh, sorry), while Dolly still looks like an inflatable rubber doll. . . . *Nine to Five* might easily have been called *The Dead End Kids Meet Gloria Steinem.* . . .

Vincent Canby, *New York Times*: "A secretary is not a toy," Frank Loesser proclaimed not too convincingly but most melodically in his hit Broadway musical, *How to Succeed in Business Without Really Trying.* Now, nearly 20 years later, we have *Nine to Five,* a comedy that turns that classic refrain into a militant cry for freedom.

Forget the energy crisis, inflation, recession, job shortages. . . . There's no problem with capitalism that three liberated Nancy Drews can't solve if they don't have to keep running out to get coffee for their bosses.

Ms. Fonda plays Judy Bernly who, recently divorced from a husband who ran off with his secretary, is taking her first job. She's the office innocent. Ms. Tomlin is Violet Newstead, the widowed mother of four, an efficient office supervisor whose promotions always go to men whom she's trained and who don't measure up to her anklebones. Ms. Parton is Doralee Rhodes, the boss' executive secretary who wears sweaters two sizes too small and pretends to be utterly surprised when men make passes at her.

Nine to Five begins as satire, slips into farce and concludes by waving the flag of feminism earnestly. Ms. Fonda is an expert comedienne but the character of Judy Bernly is much too capable to seem especially comic. . . . Considering the militancy of *Nine to Five,* it may be fitting that the funniest performance in the film is given by Dabney Coleman, who plays Franklin Hart, Jr., the dishonest, sexist boss of the company. Franklin is a lunatic villain, a mini-brained tomcat totally in the grip of his petty passions.

Meri Lyndon, *Hollywood Studio*: Good comedies are all too rare these days, and comedies which make a point and manage to enlighten and entertain an audience at the same time are rarer still. One of the sharpest, funniest, most dazzling comedies in years is *Nine to Five,* the brainchild of Jane Fonda and her increasingly busy production company, IPC. It is to her credit that she fully shares the movie with her female cohorts. . . . Each character is nicely drawn, and the numerous laughs never come at the expense of their believability or their very real predicaments. . . .

A pat on the back to Ms. Fonda, an actress whose skills improve with age (as do her remarkable looks), and who isn't content to take the scripts handed to her and simply pick out the best of the worst. As a feminist and a creative filmmaker, she is doing more for actresses, female characters and humanist entertainment than most of the studios put together.

On Golden Pond

ITC Films/IPC Films, 1981 (distributed by AFD). Directed by Mark Rydell. Produced by Bruce Gilbert. Screenplay by Ernest Thompson. From the play by Ernest Thompson.
PRINCIPAL CAST: *Katharine Hepburn, Henry Fonda, Jane Fonda, Doug Mckeon, Dabney Coleman and William Lanteau.*

If only because of its sterling cast, *On Golden Pond* was bound to be a notable movie. It marked the first teaming of Jane and Henry Fonda, as well as the first teaming of Kate and Hank, two American institutions, who'd made few films during the 1970s. For the distinguished Hepburn, it was the first released motion picture since *Rooster Cogburn and the Lady,* with the late John Wayne. (In the interval, she'd made a picture titled *Olly Olly Oxen Free,* which was never released; eventually purchased for TV showing, it has since remained on the shelf.)

In the seventies, Hank Fonda made fewer films than usual, too many of them low grade and unworthy of his talent. He and Jane had been slated to work together in *The Journey of Simon McKeever,* in which he would have starred and she would have done a cameo role as a physician, but that film was never made. *On Golden Pond* is basically the story of an elderly couple facing death. It came and went on Broadway—a touching, warm, and evocative story by Ernest Thompson, a talented young playwright. (Thompson also authored *West Side Waltz,* which Hepburn chose for her return to the stage in 1981.)

On Golden Pond didn't boast a single "young" character except thirteen-year-old Billy Ray (played by Doug Mckeon). It is unlikely, then, that *On Golden Pond* would have resurfaced as a major motion picture, had it not been for the younger Fonda's participation, which guaranteed respectable publicity and box-office returns. The movie is a co-production of England's ITC Films and Jane's IPC Films, a growing, quality force in the film industry.

The film's two main characters are Ethel and Norman Thayer. Ethel is a seventy-ish New Englander, still attractive, bursting with intelligence and vitality (who else but Kate Hepburn could have played her?). Norman is nearly eighty, less healthy and robust, occasionally lapsing into senility, and taking medication for his unstable condition. His time is limited, and both know it; they arrive at Golden Pond to spend the summer, as usual. . . . The plot is minimal; yet the household happenings and conversations, and the love shared by this noble but very human couple, are riveting and delightful.

Jane Fonda plays the Thayers' independent, forty-two-year-old daughter Chelsea, who is divorced and involved with a man named Bill Ray, a pseudo-intellectual dentist (played by Dabney Coleman, last seen as Jane's chauvinist boss in *Nine to Five*). Bill has a precocious son, whom his ex-wife isn't interested in rearing herself. Chelsea, Bill, and Billy arrive at Golden Pond, where Billy is deposited with her parents while Chelsea and Bill head for Europe and marriage.

The wry, crusty Norman and the flippant Billy eventually come to understand and appreciate each other, then regretfully part when Chelsea and Bill return and move their household to California. Summer ends, and over the phone, Ethel and Norman tentatively agree to visit Chelsea and her new family after resettling in their new Florida home. Preparing to depart, Norman stands helplessly by while Ethel loads their things into the car. Frustrated, he tries to be helpful and lifts a box of china, which he drops in the midst of a mild attack. Ethel gives him his medication and consoles him, before the couple walks out to the lake, to bid their annual, and probably final, goodbye to Golden Pond.

"It was heaven," said Jane of this cherished moviemaking experience. "Working with not one but two such tremendous talents was wonderful, inspiring. It made me be better, just by their example—and I think this is among their very best work." Besides having always wanted to work with her father in film (they'd worked together on stage, before Jane had definitely decided on an acting career), she had long admired Katharine Hepburn—perhaps the most respected living actress, a symbol of emancipated womanhood since the beginning of her fifty-year movie career. Unlike Jane (or even Bette Davis), Kate hadn't gone through a bleached-blond, vampish phase. She started out a huge talent with uncompromisingly high standards, ahead of her time in many ways, leading an independent, highly individual, very private life.

Hepburn said that Jane reminded her of herself at a younger age and that Jane was her preferred younger actress. As for Henry Fonda, he's never made a secret of the fact that he is "in awe of" his daughter.

Insiders that feel *On Golden Pond* is a sure bet to win nominations for both Kate (who's won three statuettes) and Hank, who—incredibly—has never won and whose last chance this may be to win that richly deserved token of esteem and respect. At any rate, *On Golden Pond* seems a likely film classic and a once-in-a-lifetime teaming of three of America's finest performers.

Homecoming for Chelsea and her lover's son, Billy. (Katharine Hepburn, Jane Fonda, Doug McKeon.)

Father and daughter in the film. (The first time Henry and Jane Fonda have appeared together on the screen.)

Ethel Thayer comforts her troubled daughter, Chelsea. (Katharine Hepburn and Jane Fonda.)

Jane Fonda and the Future

BESIDES BEING WIDELY CONSIDERED the best actress in America, Jane Fonda is perhaps the busiest. She now averages two films a year, although other superstars like Streisand, Beatty, and Redford make one picture every two or more years. After completing *Nine to Five,* Jane took a few months off for R and R, and political activism under the aegis of the Campaign for Economic Democracy. She also caught up with her father's ongoing theatrical career and helped celebrate his seventy-fifth birthday.

Late in 1980, her fondest professional wish, acting at last with Henry Fonda, came true, in the film version of the American play *On Golden Pond.* The two most illustrious Fondas joined Katharine Hepburn for location shooting at a lakeside manor in New Hampshire. Jane had bought the screen rights with the intent of co-starring with the two American institutions; the picture was an IPC production. (IPC Films had already changed its name to International Pictures Corp.)

Her future reportedly includes a "pay-or-play" deal for *Her Brother's Keeper,* in which she plays a female prison guard; the deal indicates she will retain a majority of the record (for an actress) two-million-dollar salary, whether or not she finally does the film (which may be re-titled.

Fonda and John Travolta have expressed a mutual wish to work together. However, after the failure of *Moment by Moment* (in which Travolta played a young man in a relationship with an older woman, portrayed by Lily Tomlin), such a collaboration is not at all certain.

In early 1981 the double Oscar winner will star in Orion's *Roll-over,* described as a "contemporary suspense thriller."

On the television front, Jane still plans to make her dramatic TV debut in *The Dollmaker,* a miniseries about a woman struggling to support her family during the Great Depression. Some insiders say *Dollmaker* is her attempt at a companion piece for *The Grapes of Wrath.* At any rate, the actress has much of her best work ahead of her, and her example and influence have almost single-handedly improved the quantity and quality of major movie roles for over-forty actresses. Like Miss Jean Brody, Ms. Jane Fonda is very much in her prime.

It is not inconceivable that the superstar may add Senator's wife to her many life roles, and if Tom Hayden wins California's 1982 elections, it would be partly because of his wife's unflagging efforts. Numerous articles in magazines like *Esquire, New West,* and *Mother Jones* have attempted to assess Hayden's political strength. Most agree that he is a formidable contender and that the CED is a growing political base for liberal reforms. The grudging admiration, right-wing potshots, and cute labels like "the Mork and Mindy of the New Left" cannot obscure the fact that Hayden is one of the best-organized "young" politicians who strongly appeal to individuals concerned with the conservative–born-again backlash.

There may shortly be a third generation of acting Fondas, for daughter Vanessa has expressed interest in a possible acting career; the teenager may make her film debut in 1981 or 1982, independently of Mama Jane. . . .

As this book goes to press, Jane Fonda is at work on her thirty-fourth film, Rollover. *In this very much cast-against-type romantic adventure story, she plays Lee Winters, former film star, now a widowed heiress to a petrochemical empire. She becomes involved with Hub Smith (Kris Kristofferson), maverick banker and troubleshooter. Between them they have everything they need to collaborate on the most daring scheme of their lives. In this still, Lee and Hub are in the early days of their relationship*